UNRAVELING ENIGMAS: 101 UNSOLVED MYSTERIES FROM ANCIENT TO MODERN TIMES

Mind-Blowing Historical, Scientific, and Paranormal Mysteries for Teens and Young Adults

Cozy Nook Books

© Copyright 2024 - All rights reserved.

The content contained within this book may not be reproduced, duplicated or transmitted without direct written permission from the author or the publisher.

Under no circumstances will any blame be placed on or legal responsibility held against the publisher or author for any damages, reparation, or monetary loss due to the information contained within this book, either directly or indirectly.

Legal Notice:

This book is copyright protected. It is only for personal use. You cannot amend, distribute, sell, use, quote or paraphrase any part of the content within this book, without the consent of the author or publisher.

Disclaimer Notice:

Please note the information contained within this document is for educational and entertainment purposes only. All effort has been executed to present accurate, up to date, reliable, complete information. No warranties of any kind are declared or implied. Readers acknowledge that the author is not engaged in the rendering of legal, financial, medical or professional advice. The content within this book has been derived from various sources. Please consult a licensed professional before attempting any techniques outlined in this book.

By reading this document, the reader agrees that under no circumstances is the author responsible for any losses, direct or indirect, that are incurred as a result of the use of the information contained within this document, including, but not limited to, errors, omissions, or inaccuracies.

TABLE OF CONTENTS

Introduction 7
Chapter 1: Ancient Mysteries.. 9
   001. Atlantis 9
   002. The Baghdad Battery 10
   003. The Voynich Manuscript 11
   004. The Antikythera Mechanism 12
   005. The Pyramids of Giza 14
   006. The Moai Statues of Easter Island 16
   007. Stonehenge 17
   008. The Sacsayhuamán Walls 18
   009. The Dead Sea Scrolls 19
   010. The Phaistos Disc 20
   011. The Great Sphinx of Giza 21
   012. The Emerald Tablet 23
   013. The Hanging Gardens of Babylon 24
   014. King Tut's Curse 25
   015. Göbekli Tepe 26
   016. The Sea Peoples 27
   017. The Lost Army of Cambyses 28
   018. The Tarim Mummies 29
   019. The Ark of the Covenant 31
   020. The Tomb of China's First Emperor 32
   021. The Dogon and the Sirius Mystery 33
   022. The Richat Structure 34
   023. The Lost Cities of Sodom and Gomorrah 35
   024. The 24 Stone Coffins of Saqqara 36
   025. The Bimini Road 37

   026. The Olmec Colossal Heads 38
   027. The Nazca Lines 39
   028. The Holy Grail 40
   029. Lost Civilizations 42

Chapter 2: Historical Mysteries 45
   030. The Mystery of the Mary Celeste 45
   031. The Disappearance of the Roanoke Colony 46
   032. The Lost City of Z 47
   033. Jack the Ripper 48
   034. The Princes in The Tower 50
   035. The Piri Reis Map 50
   036. The Green Children of Woolpit 52
   037. The Man in the Iron Mask 53
   038. The Dancing Plague of 1518 54
   039. The Lost Ship of the Colorado Desert 55
   040. The Amber Room 56
   041. The Tomb of Genghis Khan 57
   042. El Dorado 58
   043. The MV Joyita Ghost Ship 60
   044. The Miracle of the Sun 61
   045. The Oak Island Money Pit 62
   046. The Loretto Chapel Staircase 63
   047. The Codex Gigas 64
   048. The Fate of the Knights Templar 65

Chapter 3: Modern Mysteries 67
   049. The Bermuda Triangle 67
   050. The Zodiac Killer 68
   051. The Georgia Guidestones 69
   052. The Dyatlov Pass Incident 71

053. Amelia Earhart's Last Flight 72
054. The Past Life of Dorothy Eady 73
055. The Disappearance of Ambrose Bierce 74
056. The Tunguska Event 75
057. The Babushka Lady 76
058. The Mad Gasser of Mattoon 77
059. The Disappearance of Judge Crater 78
060. The Sleeping Sickness 79
061. The Circleville Letters 80
062. The Disappearance of DB Cooper 81
063. The Black Dahlia Murder 83
064. The Hopkinsville Goblins 84
065. The Somerton Man 85
066. The Disappearance of Jimmy Hoffa 86
067. The Gardner Museum Heist 87
068. The Lead Masks Case 88
069. The Coral Castle 89
070. The Mystery of Elisa Lam 90
071. The Pollock Twins 91
072. The Oakville Blobs 92
073. Flight MH370 93

Chapter 4: Scientific Mysteries 95
074. Dark Matter and Dark Energy 95
075. The Wow! Signal 96
076. The Fermi Paradox 97
077. The Flyby Anomaly 99
078. The Kuiper Cliff 100
079. The Solar Corona Mystery 101
080. The Missing Baryon Problem 102

- 081. The Theory of Everything 103
- 082. The Origin of Fast Radio Bursts 105
- 083. Early Supermassive Black Holes 106
- 084. Ball Lightning 107
- 085. The Lithium Problem 108
- 086. The Origins of UHECRs 109
- 087. The Birth of Plate Tectonics 110
- 088. The Cambrian Explosion 111
- 089. The Origins of the Moon 113
- 090. Periodic Mass Extinctions 114

Chapter 5: Cryptids, Paranormal, and Other Mysteries 116
- 091. Bigfoot 116
- 092. Out-of-Body Experiences 117
- 093. The Shroud of Turin 118
- 094. J'Ba Fofi 119
- 095. The Overtoun Bridge 120
- 096. Mokele-Mbembe 121
- 097. The Taos Hum 123
- 098. The Giant Snake of the Congo 123
- 099. The Phantom Island of Bermeja 125
- 100. Remote Viewing 126
- 101. The Loch-Ness Monster 127

Conclusion 129
References 132

INTRODUCTION

Every question has an answer. Until it doesn't—and then, it becomes a mystery!

Of course, not all mysteries are created equal. There are the small ones that poke at your mind during the day: Why did the neighbor's dog bark so much last night? What was in the school cafeteria's mystery stew today? What did Mr. Perkins say to Colin during recess that got the model student so riled up the whole afternoon? And where did that missing pair of shoes end up anyway? Perplexing though these little mysteries can be, you will not be finding them in the pages of this book.

Here you will find the big mysteries that haunt so many, even entire nations, for untold spans of time. Some have emerged only in recent times, as we learn more about the world we live in, because just as every question has an answer, every answer has a tendency to spawn even more questions. Other mysteries have eluded us for hundreds and even thousands of years. It is these grand mysteries that you will discover within the pages to come. A hundred and one of them, to be precise!

Some of these are fairly popular as mysteries go, from the Pyramids of Egypt to the Bermuda Triangle. Most may not be quite as infamous but they are just as beguiling, from the masterfully built Sacsayhuamán Walls of Peru to the mysterious Taos Hum from somewhere within the depths of the Earth.

So what is in store for you in the chapters that follow? We will begin our journey in the distant past of more than a thousand years ago. Great constructions whose origins are lost to time will rub shoulders with strange artifacts whose stories may never be known in their entirety. While we then move through the centuries toward modern times, we will learn about cities that were strangely lost, ships that were strangely found, and people who left their mark on history without a clue to their identity.

As we enter the 20th century, we will catch a fleeting glimpse of famous personalities, such as aviator Amelia Earhart and union leader Jimmy Hoffa—and see how they disappeared without a trace. Strange events will abound, from the explosion in Tunguska to the disappearance of flight MH370. We will then enter the present day with a look at the biggest scientific mysteries that still boggle the greatest minds of our times. Finally, we will veer into the world of the paranormal, where cryptids like the Yeti and the Loch Ness monster roam—along with even more unexplained curiosities.

So sit back, dust off your adventuring hat, and prepare to unravel and enjoy some of the most intriguing enigmas our world has to offer. And remember that for every mystery in these pages, there are many that were eventually solved by keen and inquiring minds like yours. Perhaps the you that exists many years from now will be the one to solve some of these puzzles—who knows? After all, the biggest mystery that has hounded humanity throughout our brief time here is what the future will bring…

CHAPTER 1:
ANCIENT MYSTERIES

001. Atlantis

A grand and flourishing city, the center of a great empire, all struck down by forces of nature and lost to the depths of the Atlantic Ocean—but what was the true nature of Atlantis?

According to the ancient Greek philosopher Plato, Atlantis was a powerful and advanced civilization that existed over 11,000 years ago. In his dialogues *Timaeus* and *Critias*, he described Atlantis as a wonderful utopia that ultimately fell out of favor with the gods due to the arrogance and pride of its people. The grand, flourishing city was then submerged beneath the sea, vanishing from sight in a single day and night!

But did Atlantis actually exist? While this has not been confirmed by archaeological evidence so far, some researchers believe that Plato may have been inspired by real events—involving a real place. In 1600 BCE, a volcanic eruption destroyed the island of Santorini in the Aegean Sea near Greece; the demise of the island has a lot in common with Plato's description of the fate of Atlantis.

Even where Atlantis was located remains one of the greatest unsolved mysteries of our time. Theories place it anywhere from the depths of the Atlantic Ocean (which was *not* named after the mythical city, but instead takes its name from the Greek Titan Atlas) to regions as far apart as the Antarctic Ocean and the Mediterranean Sea.

Over the years, Atlantis has become a staple of popular culture, appearing in many books, movies, and TV shows, from Disney's animated film *Atlantis: The Lost Empire* to Jules Verne's classic novel

Twenty Thousand Leagues Under the Sea. But despite decades of speculation and exploration, the search for Atlantis continues.

Modern technologies like sonar and satellite imaging have allowed researchers to scour the ocean floor in search of the ruins of ancient civilizations. But while some promising discoveries have been made, none of them have turned out to be concrete proof of Atlantis's existence.

So what was the true nature of the lost continent of Atlantis? Some believe it to be part of a metaphorical tale created by Plato, a model society that he used to discuss philosophy. Others think it was a real civilization (given some exaggerated flair by the Greek philosopher, as his type sometimes did!) that met a tragic end. Still, some people speculate that Atlantis may have been a highly advanced society, with knowledge and technology far beyond its time—and maybe even ours! Whatever it may have been, Atlantis continues to inspire wonder and curiosity, and its legacy is a reminder of humanity's endless quest for knowledge and discovery.

002. The Baghdad Battery

Did the ancient Mesopotamians create electricity?

The Baghdad Battery was discovered in the ruins of Khujut Rabu near Baghdad, Iraq in the 1930s. Inside these ruins, archaeologists stumbled upon an astonishing find: an earthenware jar containing a copper cylinder, an iron rod, and traces of what could have been vinegar or wine. While that may not sound too exciting in itself, what made this discovery truly captivating was that the design of the jar suggested it could have been used as a battery. Imagine—electricity in the ancient world!

Dating back to around 250 BCE to 224 CE during the Parthian period, this find raises many questions about what the ancients were technologically capable of. The Baghdad Battery operated on a simple principle: an acidic solution (the vinegar or wine) could act as an electrolyte between the copper cylinder and iron rod. Put together, this would allow the device to generate a small electric current. While it wouldn't be enough to power today's smartphones, it could have served various other purposes, from primitive medicine to religious displays.

The fact that the Baghdad Battery even existed hints at what could have been a scientifically advanced society in ancient Mesopotamia. This region has often been called the "Cradle of Civilization," because it was the birthplace of many remarkable ideas in mathematics, astronomy, and engineering. Could the people of that time have been ingenious enough to invent a battery? Very likely! But did they actually do so?

As with most historical mysteries, other theories have been suggested. Some think the Baghdad Battery didn't generate electricity at all, and was instead used to coat jewelry or money with precious metals, or for therapeutic purposes. But these theories don't fully explain the battery's design and components—and definitive proof about the battery's purpose continues to elude us to this day.

003. The Voynich Manuscript

The Voynich Manuscript was found by antique book dealer Wilfrid Voynich in a collection of manuscripts purchased in 1912 from the Society of Jesus in Italy. Dating back to the early 15th century CE (Common Era), this mysterious document is written in an unknown script or language, and the words are accompanied by intricate drawings of plants, celestial bodies, and even fantastical scenes.

One of the most baffling puzzles in the Voynich Manuscript is its indecipherable script. Linguists and cryptographers over the years have tried to unlock its secrets, but none have succeeded. Is it a lost language, a complex cipher, or an elaborate hoax?

Just as the text defies interpretation, so too are the detailed illustrations. Strange plants, astrological charts, and surreal human figures are scattered among its pages. Some think these drawings hold the clues to finding the manuscript's hidden meaning, while others believe they are just for show.

The origin of the Voynich Manuscript remains just as shrouded in mystery as its contents. Theories have connected it to medieval alchemists, and even the infamous Renaissance polymath Leonardo da Vinci—it wouldn't be the only time the genius wrote and illustrated a deeply confounding manuscript! Others suggest it could have been a 16th-century forgery or a hoax of a similar kind.

Various scientific techniques from carbon dating to spectroscopy have been used to analyze the Voynich Manuscript. Thanks to these, we know the age of the manuscript and what materials are in it, but science can't yet figure out its content or purpose.

So what could the Voynich Manuscript be about? Some believe it is a medical or herbal compendium, while others think it contains alchemical recipes or astrological information. But without a key to unlock its code, these theories remain conjecture, and the secrets of the manuscript remain hidden, waiting to be uncovered by a future generation.

004. The Antikythera Mechanism

The ancient Greeks were one of the great civilizations of the past. But were they capable of creating a device that could accurately model our solar system?

The Antikythera Mechanism was discovered in 1901 by Greek sponge divers exploring a shipwreck near the island of Antikythera. In the wreckage, they found a corroded bronze artifact that was, at first, simple yet intriguing, but then broke apart to reveal an astonishing feat of ancient engineering inside!

What makes the Antikythera Mechanism so fascinating is its intricate design. It has a large number of gears and dials, and the device as a whole looks like a complex clockwork mechanism. But its true purpose remained a mystery for decades until researchers determined, through careful and thorough study, that the Antikythera Mechanism was in fact an astronomical calculator. Dating back to the 2nd century BCE, it would have been used to track the movements of stars and planets, and could even help to predict astronomical events like eclipses.

The clever construction of the Antikythera Mechanism challenges what we thought we knew about ancient technology. Its nested gears that could even roughly model the orbits of planets, and the precision of its engineering, point to a level of craftsmanship never seen before in the ancient world. It is in many ways a primitive computer; how were the Greeks able to craft and assemble it without the kind of modern tools we need to construct similar devices today?

Inscriptions and markings were also found on the Antikythera Mechanism, and figuring these out has been a monumental task for historians and scientists over the years. While we have learned much about how it works, such as how it could calculate the positions of planets over time, many questions still remain. How was it constructed? Who built it? And why was such a sophisticated device even made in the first place? These gaps in our knowledge may someday be filled by future exploration and further study.

005. The Pyramids of Giza

It took the blood, sweat, and tears of thousands of men to build these magnificent marvels of the ancient world, but is there more to these monuments than we already know?

On the outskirts of modern-day Cairo, Egypt, looming above the desert sands on the west bank of the River Nile, sit some of the most iconic and enduring symbols of ancient civilization: the Pyramids of Giza. Built over 4,500 years ago, during the reign of pharaohs Khufu, Khafre, and Menkaure, these grand tombs stand to this day as monuments of the power and ambition of ancient Egyptian civilization.

The Great Pyramid of Khufu, the largest of the three pyramids, originally stood at an awe-inspiring height of 481 feet—if it was a high-rise building, it would have more than 30 floors. Constructed using millions of limestone blocks, each block was precisely cut and fitted without the use of mortar or cement, a testament to the advanced skills of those ancient Egyptian engineers; the blocks are so carefully placed together that not even a hair can fit in the gaps between the stones!

Despite centuries of study, the exact methods that were used to transport the heavy stone blocks from the quarry to the construction sites and then construct the pyramids themselves are still debated among historians and archaeologists. Theories range from the use of simple ramps and levers in ingenious ways to the use of advanced scientific principles together with armies of coordinated labor to make complex maneuvers much easier to perform. Some have even suggested that extraterrestrials or magicians were involved in the construction!

One of the most intriguing aspects of the Pyramids of Giza is that they are very precisely placed and oriented; the sides of the Great Pyramid are lined up with the four cardinal directions (North, South, East, and West) with remarkable accuracy, and even its internal chambers are thought to face or be aligned toward specific stars and constellations.

Ancient Egyptians believed in a far more complex afterlife than most of today's religions. Originally intended as tombs for the pharaohs and their queens, the pyramids were designed to protect the valuable royal remains from grave robbers and thieves, and ensure the pharaoh's smooth journey through the afterlife. Although ancient tomb raiders eventually managed to break in and plunder many of these valuables, the pyramids still contain remnants of their majestic past—from burial chambers to religious artifacts.

As symbols of ancient Egypt's grandeur and achievement, the Pyramids of Giza hold a special place in world history and culture. Their mysterious allure continues to draw millions of visitors each year to gaze upon their timeless beauty and wonder what yet-to-be-discovered secrets might lie within these extraordinary structures.

006. The Moai Statues of Easter Island

They have stood guard around their home for thousands of years, with their absurdly large heads and vacant stares. But how did the Moai come to be?

Rapa Nui, as it is known to its inhabitants, is a remote island in the vastness of the Pacific Ocean, surrounded only by water. To the rest of the world, it is known as Easter Island, a small, isolated patch of land on which stand the enigmatic Moai, monolithic human figures carved by the Rapa Nui people.

More than 900 of the colossal stone figures with disproportionately large heads were placed around the island by the Rapa Nui people centuries ago. These awe-inspiring sculptures range in height from a few feet tall to more than 30 feet high. The tallest of these, named "Paro," is 33 feet high and weighs 82 tons!

Crafted from volcanic tuff, which is formed when the ash from a volcanic eruption becomes solid and naturally compresses over time, the Moai are indicative of the remarkable skill and precision of their makers. But how did the Rapa Nui people, with limited resources and tools, and on an island far away from the rest of civilization, manage to create so many grand masterpieces?

One of the greatest mysteries surrounding the Moai is how they were transported across the island from the quarry where they were carved. Some believe the statues were walked upright using a method of rocking and swiveling the figures known as "walking the Moai," while others suggest they were moved horizontally on sledges or rolled on logs. The techniques used by the ancient islanders (who wouldn't have had large numbers to make their task easier) continue to elude those who study them.

What drove the Rapa Nui people to build these imposing statues? Some theories suggest they were erected to honor their ancestors, or to serve as guardians or markers for sacred sites. Others think they symbolize authority or royal lineage, and were tied to the social and political dynamics of the Rapa Nui people. Whatever the answer, the silent presence of the statues serves as a reminder of a vibrant culture that was able to thrive in the middle of the ocean, leaving behind a legacy that captivates and inspires all who visit.

007. Stonehenge

Located on Salisbury Plain in Wiltshire, England, Stonehenge is a monument that dates back to prehistoric times. At its heart lies a circle of towering stones, some reaching up to 30 feet in height and weighing as much as 25 tons. These colossal stones have stood for thousands of years, silently guarding secrets of the past.

One of the most famous features of Stonehenge is its alignment with the sunrise on the summer solstice (the longest day of the year) as well as with the sunset of the winter solstice (the shortest day of the year). Every June, thousands of people gather at Stonehenge to witness the sunrise over the heel stone that marks the beginning of summer. The solstice celebrations highlight the fascination and spiritual significance of this ancient site.

The construction of Stonehenge is a puzzle that has baffled historians and archaeologists for centuries. How did the people who lived there around 2500 BCE transport these massive stones over long distances? How were these stones arranged with such precision, and without the aid of modern technology? The answers continue to elude us, adding to the mystique of this ancient site.

Over the years, many theories have attempted to explain the purpose of Stonehenge. Some believe, based on the other remains that have been found at the site, that it served as a burial ground, while others suggest it was a kind of astronomical observatory or a sacred site for religious ceremonies (which might explain why it is lined up with the sun). But despite centuries of study, these questions and others about Stonehenge remain unanswered. Who built it, and why? What was its true function?

Stonehenge may have survived for thousands of years, and worked its way into all manner of pop culture and folklore legends, but it is not immune to the effects of time and human activity. Efforts are being made to preserve this iconic monument and ensure that its secrets will continue to inspire wonder and curiosity for years to come.

008. The Sacsayhuamán Walls

The Inca people are an underrated civilization when we think about what they achieved. The Sacsayhuamán Walls, nestled high above the city of Cusco, Peru, stand as a testament to the ingenuity and skill of the ancient Inca civilization in South America.

The walls are made of colossal limestone blocks, with some weighing upwards of 300 tons, and stretch out to over 1,000 feet in total length, with some sections rising to heights of nearly 20 feet—quite the sight to behold!

The construction of the Sacsayhuamán Walls is a marvel of engineering that continues to baffle historians and archaeologists to this day. How did the Inca people quarry, transport, and fit these massive stones together with such precision, and without the use of modern tools or machinery? The blocks are not all of a regular shape, yet they seamlessly fit together in place along the walls. The sheer scale and complexity of the construction are nothing short of astonishing.

There are many legends about the construction of the Sacsayhuamán Walls, with some claiming they were built by giants or extraterrestrial beings. While these stories add to the mystique of the site, the truth behind their creation lies in the ingenuity and labor of the thousands of Inca builders who meticulously carved and placed each stone by hand, according to chroniclers from the Spanish conquistadors who were in the region during the 16th century CE.

The Sacsayhuamán Walls are likely to have served a strategic purpose for the Inca Empire. They are positioned on a hill overlooking the city of Cusco, and surround the remains of what could have been a fortress or ceremonial center, offering protection and prestige to the ruling elite within.

Today, the Sacsayhuamán Walls are a symbol of Peruvian national pride and their rich cultural heritage. Efforts are underway to protect the Sacsayhuamán Walls from erosion, vandalism, and the ravages of time. By studying both these structures and the surrounding archaeological sites, researchers hope to gain more insight into the daily lives, beliefs, and achievements of the Inca people.

009. The Dead Sea Scrolls

These scrolls are the work of many unknown scribes, and were found in caves near the saltiest sea in the world. What could these ancient scrolls reveal about the origins of the Bible?

The Dead Sea Scrolls are a collection of ancient manuscripts, written on parchment and papyrus, discovered in 1947 when a Bedouin shepherd stumbled upon a cave near the Dead Sea in Qumran and found clay jars filled with the ancient scrolls. These remarkably well-preserved scrolls contained some of the oldest known copies of biblical texts, such as copies of the Book of Isaiah, Psalms, and Deuteronomy, as well as non-biblical writings, including hymns, prayers, and legal documents.

After the initial discovery, archaeologists and explorers uncovered more caves in the area with clay jars, revealing more scrolls and fragments that shed light on the lives, culture, and religious beliefs of the ancient Jewish community that inhabited the region.

One of the enduring mysteries of the Dead Sea Scrolls is the identity of the authors and scribes who wrote these ancient texts. While some scholars believe they were compiled by an ancient Jewish sect known as the Essenes, others suggest they may have been the work of multiple communities living in the region from the 3rd century BCE to the 1st century CE.

Among the Scrolls, one stands out for its unique content and cryptic message: the Copper Scroll.

Unlike the others, which are written on parchment, the Copper Scroll is inscribed on sheets of thin copper. And instead of religious scripture, the Copper Scroll lists 64 locations and descriptions of hidden treasures, including gold, silver, and other valuable items, though none of these have ever been found! While some believe it to be a literal treasure map, leading to riches buried in the Judean desert, others suggest it might instead be a symbolic or allegorical text with some kind of esoteric teachings.

The discovery of the Dead Sea Scrolls was a watershed moment in the field of biblical archaeology, sparking much interest and debate. Advanced techniques such as digital imaging and DNA analysis have been used to unlock their secrets and ensure their long-term preservation. They have reshaped our understanding of the origins of Judaism and Christianity and inspired countless research projects, documentaries, and exhibitions around the world.

010. The Phaistos Disc

Before the Greeks ruled the Aegean seas, there were the Minoans, a people who were just as knowledgeable as the Greeks.

A small circular disc of fired clay, the Phaistos Disc was discovered in 1908 by Italian archaeologist Luigi Pernier at the ancient Minoan palace of Phaistos on the Mediterranean island of Crete. Dating back to the Bronze Age, this unique artifact is covered in mysterious symbols arranged in a spiral pattern on both its sides, and has captured the imagination of historians, linguists, and cryptographers alike.

The Phaistos Disc features a total of 241 pictographic symbols stamped onto both sides. These symbols range from tiny human figures and animals to geometric shapes and mysterious objects, and have so far defied all attempts made to decipher them, leaving scholars and historians intrigued as to their meaning.

One of the greatest mysteries surrounding the Phaistos Disc is the language in which it is written—assuming that it is a language in the first place. Many theories and hypotheses have been suggested, including that the disc was imprinted with a Minoan dialect, an early form of Greek, or even an alien script! But the true origins of the symbols, linguistic or otherwise, remain unknown.

What is the purpose of the disc, though? What secrets did the Minoans put inside it? Some believe it contains a hidden message or story; it could be the re-telling of a grand mythological tale or parable, a record of important historical events, or simply a religious or ceremonial object. But without a key to unlock its code, the true meaning of the symbols remains tantalizingly out of reach.

The Phaistos Disc is a testament to the mystique and ingenuity of the ancient Minoan civilization, the latter of which is clear from its intricate design. The cryptic symbols on either side of the disc represent the continued allure of the past, and secrets that wait to be revealed.

011. The Great Sphinx of Giza

Perched proudly on the Giza Plateau in Egypt, and not too far from the iconic Pyramids of Giza, the Great Sphinx is a colossal statue with the body of a lion and the head of a human. It was carved from a single large limestone block, and this majestic creature has captivated the imaginations of travelers and scholars for thousands of years. But where did it come from? And what happened to its nose?

The origins of the Great Sphinx are shrouded in mystery, and historians have debated its age and purpose for centuries. While most agree that it was built during the reign of Pharaoh Khafre around 2500 BCE (and was likely to have been built as a monument in his name), some theories, based on its level of relative erosion, suggest that it may be even older than all the pyramids, and date back to the Early Dynastic Period in Ancient Egypt (approximately 3150 BCE to 2700 BCE).

The Sphinx was a creature of myth. In ancient Egypt, it was revered as a symbol of strength, wisdom, and guardianship. The fact that it was built near the pyramids of Giza, themselves meant to guard pharaohs during their journey through the afterlife, reinforces its association with royal power and divine protection. In Greek mythology, the Sphinx was said to pose a riddle to travelers who entered its path, and devoured those who could not answer correctly. The riddle: "What has one voice but goes on four legs in the morning, two in the afternoon, and three in the evening?" was solved by Greek hero Oedipus, who answered "man," who crawls as a baby, stands on two legs as an adult, and walks with a stick in old age.

Despite its grandeur, the Great Sphinx has been weathered by the sands of time, which have obscured many of its original features. Its prominently missing nose in particular has been the subject of much speculation, with theories ranging from natural erosion to vandalism. Still, the statue stands as a symbol of Egypt's rich cultural heritage and the craftsmanship of its ancient builders, even as the exact purpose of its creation remains unknown.

012. The Emerald Tablet

The Emerald Tablet is a legendary tablet of green stone said to contain the secrets of the universe. Its content has inspired scientists and alchemists over the years, but the Tablet itself has yet to be found. What was its true nature?

According to ancient texts, it was created by the legendary figure Hermes Trismegistus, a mythical merging of the Greek messenger god Hermes and the Egyptian god Thoth, who was the "scribe of the Gods" in ancient Egyptian mythology. Emeralds are traditionally associated with Hermes in Greek mythology, along with the metal mercury, which, by the way, is the name of the god in Roman mythology who shares many features with Hermes.

The most famous phrase to come from the Emerald Tablet is "As above, so below; as below, so above." This enigmatic statement speaks to the principle of correspondence, and a profound connection between the individual parts of a whole and the sum of those parts. It also strongly implies a link between the heavens and the Earth.

The Emerald Tablet is also said to contain instructions for creating the Philosopher's Stone, a legendary substance believed to have the power to convert base metals like lead and iron into gold, and grant eternal life. The pursuit of the Philosopher's Stone was a central goal of alchemy, the ancient precursor to modern chemistry, which is why the Emerald Tablet is sometimes seen as a foundational text of alchemy.

The inscriptions from the Emerald Tablet are written in a cryptic style, filled with symbolism and allegory. Many translations of the text exist, each with a different interpretation of its teachings, ranging from the literal to the metaphorical—including one by the famous scientist (and occasional alchemist) Sir Isaac Newton!

Despite the mystery of its origins, the Emerald Tablet has inspired alchemists, philosophers, and mystics throughout history. Its teachings are said to cover a wide range of topics, from the nature of reality to the pursuit of wisdom and spiritual enlightenment.

013. The Hanging Gardens of Babylon

Bountiful gardens with green trees and sparkling water, all in the middle of the desert; did the ancient Babylonians truly create such a paradise?

The Hanging Gardens of Babylon are said to have been an extraordinary feat of engineering and gardening that were constructed in the ancient city of Babylon (near present-day Baghdad, Iraq) around 600 BCE. According to ancient accounts, these bountiful gardens with green trees and sparkling water, all in the middle of the desert, were a sight to behold, and included towering terraces filled with exotic plants and cascading waterfalls. The name comes from the Greek word *kremastós*, which loosely translates to "overhanging" and was used to describe trees that were planted on raised platforms, such as terraces.

The Hanging Gardens are thought to have been commissioned by the powerful ruler of the Neo-Babylonian Empire, King Nebuchadnezzar II, as a tribute to his queen, Amytis of Media. Legend has it that Amytis longed for the green hills and forests of her homeland, which prompted Nebuchadnezzar to create the gardens as a symbol of his love for her.

One of the greatest mysteries about the Hanging Gardens is how they were constructed. Ancient Babylon had an arid climate and flat terrain, so lush gardens and waterfalls suspended above the ground would have been quite a miracle! Some theories suggest that a series of tiered terraces were built together with a complex system of irrigation channels and aqueducts, which allowed for the soil to better support the growth of plants and trees.

Despite how grandly the Hanging Gardens are described in ancient accounts, there is a lack of concrete archaeological evidence that they actually existed. Ancient historians such as Herodotus and Strabo may have vividly described the gardens, but their writings are often based on hearsay and speculation. None of them ever viewed the place in person.

Though the physical ruins of the Hanging Gardens (or their real-life source of inspiration) may have been lost to time, they have captivated the imaginations of poets, artists, and historians for centuries and inspired countless works of art, literature, and architecture. Whether real or mythical, their legacy as a symbol of earthly paradise and human ingenuity continues to inspire wonder and awe to this day.

014. King Tut's Curse

Ancient tombs often hold many secrets inside their dusty walls, but do they also carry deadly curses?

In 1922, British archaeologist Howard Carter made a great discovery in the Valley of the Kings in Egypt: the tomb of the young pharaoh Tutankhamun, also known as King Tut. The tomb was remarkably well-preserved, and filled with treasures and artifacts unseen for thousands of years. But soon after the tomb's discovery, rumors of a curse began to spread. It was said that anyone who dared disturb the resting place of the pharaoh would suffer dire consequences like illness, accidents, and even death!

Following the opening of King Tut's tomb, a series of unexplained deaths occurred among those who had been in the excavation party, including the Earl of Carnarvon, the financial backer of the expedition, who died from a mosquito bite infection shortly after the tomb's opening. It was his death that went on to set ablaze rumors about the curse.

The legend of King Tut's Curse became a media sensation afterward, with newspapers around the world making a sensation out of the fantastical curse and fueling public interest in ancient Egypt. The stories added drama and intrigue to the discovery of King Tut's tomb and further cemented the young pharaoh's legacy.

Over the years, though, scientists have come up with rational explanations for the deaths associated with King Tut's tomb. Some have suggested that exposure to toxic molds and bacteria found inside the sealed tomb may have caused respiratory illnesses and other infections, leading to the deaths of some of those who entered.

As such, skeptics have questioned the validity of the curse, believing that the deaths were coincidence or due to natural causes. Critics propose that the curse was a product of sensationalism and superstition, stirred up by media hype and the public's fascination with the occult during that time.

While the truth behind the curse may never be known, the legend of King Tut's Curse has endured for nearly a century as a testament to the power of the occult and our continued fascination with ancient Egypt.

015. Göbekli Tepe

In 1994, German archaeologist Klaus Schmidt was surveying the Southeast Anatolia region of Turkey when he uncovered something astonishing—a complex of massive stone pillars arranged in circular formations, predating the construction of Stonehenge by thousands of years. The site of these ancient ruins came to be known as Göbekli Tepe.

In fact, Göbekli Tepe predates the advent of agriculture and settled societies by several generations, dating back 11,000 years! The find challenges what we know about the rise and development of civilization, since its construction required knowledge of stone working and communal labor that was very advanced for its time.

The site consists of several circular enclosures or rings, each with large, T-shaped pillars that have intricate carvings of animals, symbols, and humanoid figures on them. The pillars reach up to 16 feet in height and some weigh several tons; the fact that they were meticulously carved and transported from the quarry to the site is a remarkable feat for a pre-agricultural society.

What was the purpose of Göbekli Tepe? Archaeologists believe the site was a center for rituals and ceremonies, and possibly even an early form of religion. The carvings on the pillars depict animals, hunting scenes, and abstract symbols, which suggest they have some kind of spiritual significance.

In spite of this, Göbekli Tepe was mysteriously abandoned around 8000 BCE, doomed to be buried beneath layers of sediment over the years. The reasons it was abandoned remain unclear, but archaeologists have suggested changes in the environment, social upheaval, or shifts in religious beliefs.

Excavations at Göbekli Tepe continue to stimulate new insights into its origins and possible purpose. Recent discoveries around the original find have revealed more enclosures and elaborately carved pillars, adding to our understanding of this ancient site and its place in human history.

016. The Sea Peoples

During the late Bronze Age, around the 12th century BCE, and long before the rise of pirates in the Caribbean seas, the Sea Peoples first appeared. They are referred to in Egyptian historical records and other ancient texts as formidable invaders, who caused chaos and upheaval along the shores of the Mediterranean.

But who were the Sea Peoples? Their true origins and identity remain a subject of debate among historians and archaeologists. Some suggest they may have been a confederation of different ethnic groups in the region, while others propose they were displaced refugees seeking new lands and resources.

The Sea Peoples are best known for their maritime invasions and conquests during the Late Bronze Age Collapse, a modern term used to refer to the decline and fall of major Mediterranean civilizations between 1250 and 1150 BCE. They targeted major civilizations such as the Hittites, Mycenaeans, and Egyptians, and it is believed they played a key role in the downfall of these once-great empires. The Sea Peoples were skilled seafarers and warriors who used advanced naval tactics and weaponry. They had warships, including galleys and naval archers, with which they launched devastating attacks on coastal settlements and trade routes.

Ultimately, the Sea Peoples faced defeat at the hands of the Egyptian pharaoh Ramses III in the Battle of the Delta, around 1178 BCE, after which they mysteriously disappeared from historical records, leaving behind a legacy of intrigue and speculation.

The impact of the Sea Peoples' movements and assaults on the ancient world was profound. Their incursions led to the collapse of long-established civilizations, which resulted in political instability, upheavals in economics and trade, and the disintegration of societies across the Eastern Mediterranean region. The Sea Peoples' mysterious origins, formidable military prowess, and sudden disappearance continue to captivate the imagination, and their legacy inspires scholarly inquiry to this day.

017. The Lost Army of Cambyses

This tale begins in the 6th century BCE, during the reign of Cambyses II of the mighty Persian Empire. In a bid to expand the lands that he ruled, Cambyses embarked on a daring military campaign to conquer the land of Egypt, and in doing so set the stage for one of history's most perplexing disappearances.

According to ancient sources, Cambyses led a vast army intent on conquest across the Egyptian desert—as many as 50,000 men! However, as the army ventured deeper into the unforgiving desert, it is said to have vanished without a trace. All that remained of this army were whispers of their fate.

The disappearance of Cambyses' army has sparked numerous theories over the centuries. These theories include being swallowed by the treacherous sands of the desert, falling victim to hostile tribes or internal rebellion, becoming hopelessly lost on their journey, or succumbing to thirst and exhaustion, the last of which is very easy to do in the deserts of Egypt!

The ancient Greek historian Herodotus gives one of the earliest accounts of the lost army in his writings. According to him, Cambyses' soldiers were overwhelmed by a colossal sandstorm, which buried the lot of them beneath the shifting dunes, sealing their fate.

In recent years, archaeologists and explorers have tried to unravel the mystery of the Lost Army of Cambyses. Expeditions into the Egyptian desert have uncovered some tantalizing clues, including scattered artifacts and human remains. While these are not definitive proof of the thousands of warriors who vanished, they have reignited interest in this ancient mystery. The legend of the Lost Army of Cambyses lives on as a reminder of the dangers of the untamed desert, and instills wonder about what else may lie buried under its sands.

018. The Tarim Mummies

In the early 20th century, archaeologists exploring the desolate landscapes of the Tarim Basin in Xinjiang, China, stumbled upon a remarkable series of mummified human remains. Dating back over 4,000 years, these mummies offer a mystifying glimpse into the ancient cultures of the region. What sets the Tarim Mummies apart from other mummies is how exceptional their state of preservation is. Despite the passage of thousands of years, many of them still possess their skin, hair, and even clothing!

DNA analysis of the Tarim Mummies has revealed some surprising insights into their origins. Although discovered in China, many of them show features that are normally found in European and West Eurasian populations. The Tarim Basin was a key crossroads along the ancient Silk Road, a famous trade route that allowed for trade and cultural exchange between the worlds of East and West. The discovery of European-featured mummies in this remote region suggests that there were deeper connections between distant civilizations than previously thought. There may even have been migrations from one side of the continent to the other.

In addition to their genetics, the Tarim Mummies offer clues about the cultural practices of ancient Central Asian societies. Some of the mummies were found buried with elaborate textiles, intricate jewelry, and even evidence of tattoos, all of which show the richness and complexity of their cultural traditions.

An intriguing aspect of the Tarim Mummies is their possible connection to the ancient Tocharian civilization. Linguistic and archaeological evidence suggests that some of the Tarim Basin people may have spoken Tocharian languages, a branch of the Indo-European language family that mysteriously went extinct in the 9th century CE.

Despite decades of study, many questions about the Tarim Mummies remain unanswered. The origins of these people, their cultural affiliations, and the circumstances of their preservation continue to puzzle researchers and fuel inquiry.

019. The Ark of the Covenant

The Ten Commandments, one of the foundations of the Christian faith, were engraved in stone tablets. But what happened to these tablets?

The story of the Ark of the Covenant can be traced back to ancient Israelite tradition, as described in the Hebrew Bible known as the Tanakh. According to scripture, the ark was a sacred chest made of wood overlaid with gold that housed the stone tablets inscribed with the Ten Commandments that were given to Moses on Mount Sinai.

The Ark was also believed to be blessed with divine power, serving as a symbol of God's presence among the Israelites. It was carried by them during their 40 years of wandering in the desert and played a central role in religious rituals and ceremonies, including the Battle of Jericho.

The fate of the Ark of the Covenant remains shrouded in mystery. According to biblical accounts, it was eventually placed in the First Temple of Jerusalem built by King Solomon. But after the temple was destroyed by the Babylonians in 586 BCE, the ark disappeared without a trace.

Over the centuries, numerous theories and legends have emerged about the fate of the Ark. Some say it was hidden away in a secret chamber beneath the Old City in Jerusalem, while others suggest it was taken by the Babylonians as spoils of war. There are even claims that it was spirited away to Ethiopia along the river Nile.

The Ark of the Covenant has captured the imagination of popular culture, appearing in films, novels, and video games. It was famously depicted in the movie *Raiders of the Lost Ark* as a powerful artifact sought after by professor of archaeology Indiana Jones, as well as treasure hunters and Nazis alike.

Despite the lack of concrete evidence, archaeological expeditions continue to search for the Ark. Some believe it may still be hidden within the Temple Mount, a holy site in Jerusalem, waiting to be discovered beneath layers of ancient rubble. Whether it lies hidden in a forgotten chamber or was lost to the sands of time, the legend of the Ark of the Covenant still mystifies and inspires many today, who are enthralled by the power of ancient relics and the quest for truth.

020. The Tomb of China's First Emperor

China's first emperor, Qin Shi Huang, was a formidable ruler who unified the country in 221 BCE and established the Qin Dynasty. Renowned for his ambition and ruthlessness, Qin Shi Huang oversaw the construction of the Great Wall and the standardization of laws, currency, and writing systems in ancient China.

In death, Qin Shi Huang spared no expense to ensure his legacy. He had a vast mausoleum constructed near modern-day Xi'an, complete with a terracotta army to guard his tomb and accompany him into the afterlife. The army was comprised of more than 130 horse-drawn chariots, 150 cavalry soldiers, and 8,000 warriors.

According to ancient accounts from Chinese historian Sima Qian, the tomb is said to be protected by ingenious booby traps designed to thwart any grave robbers or intruders. Legends and accounts speak of hidden pitfalls, poison gases, rivers of toxic mercury, and even crossbow traps lying in wait for those who dared disturb the emperor's slumber!

The discovery of the iconic terracotta army in 1974 offered the world's first glimpse into Qin Shi Huang's vast necropolis. Thousands of life-sized clay soldiers, each with unique facial features and armor, were found standing guard over the emperor's burial site. While there have been many excavations around the site, Qin Shi Huang's actual tomb remains unopened, as archaeologists have been concerned about damaging the artifacts inside, and also about the risk of triggering any extra traps hidden within.

In recent years, though, advances in archaeological technology, such as ground-penetrating radar and Lidar (Light Detection and Ranging, a remote sensing method that uses light in the form of a pulsed laser to measure variable distances to the Earth) scanning have allowed researchers to look beneath the surface of the complex without disturbing its contents or foundations. These non-invasive techniques might lead to new insights about the tomb's layout and construction as the exploration continues, as well as reveal more about what secrets lie in the tomb of Emperor Qin Shi Huang.

021. The Dogon and the Sirius Mystery

The Dogon, an indigenous ethnic group living in Mali in West Africa, are known for their rich cultural heritage and unique traditions, such as their mask dances. Among their most intriguing beliefs is their vast knowledge of the stars, passed down from their ancestors through oral tradition and sacred rituals.

The second half of this mystery involves Sirius, the brightest star in the night sky and a beacon of the cosmos revered by ancient cultures around the world. Known as the "Dog Star," Sirius holds a special significance in Dogon cosmology (where it is known as *Sigi Tolo*), as it represents knowledge, wisdom, and spiritual enlightenment. In their creation myth, the Dogon people believed that the Dog Star was home to the mythical *Nommo*, amphibious beings resembling mermaids sent by the creator god *Amma* to impart knowledge and wisdom to humanity.

What truly sets the Dogon apart, though, is their remarkably detailed understanding of Sirius and its star system long before humans began to use telescopes and other astronomical instruments. For example, Dogon mythology speaks of two invisible companion stars that orbit around Sirius. Modern technology was only able to confirm the presence of these stars, known as Sirius B and Sirius C, centuries later!

The Dogon's knowledge of Sirius has sparked controversy among scholars and skeptics. Some argue that it could not have been obtained without outside influence, in other words, from ancient astronauts or extraterrestrial beings.

Despite the speculation, most anthropologists agree that the Dogon's understanding of Sirius was passed down through the generations by way of oral storytelling and ritual observations of the night sky. Their surprisingly intricate cosmology reflects humanity's deep connection to the natural world and the cosmos, and their ancient wisdom inspires wonder and curiosity among scholars everywhere.

022. The Richat Structure

The Richat Structure, also known as the "Eye of the Sahara," was first seen in its entirety by early space travelers orbiting Earth. Seen from above, its concentric rings and striking patterns resemble a bull's eye on an archery target. It wasn't until satellite imagery became more established that scientists could begin to study in detail the sheer scale of this natural marvel.

The Richat Structure is a massive circular formation in the Adrar Plateau of the Sahara, spanning approximately 30 miles in diameter—a massive bull's eye indeed! Its distinct concentric rings are made up of sedimentary rocks like limestone, dolomite, and quartzite, sculpted over millions of years by erosion and other geological processes.

The exact origin of the Richat Structure remains a subject of debate among geologists. While some think it was formed by an ancient volcanic eruption or meteorite impact, others believe it is the result of erosion and uplift caused by tectonic forces.

Regardless of how it came to be, the Richat Structure's natural beauty is plain to see even from the ground. Its geometric patterns, rugged terrain, and vibrant colors are a sight to behold, and the otherworldly landscape around it has even drawn comparisons to the surface of Mars. The Richat Structure also holds cultural significance for the indigenous peoples of the Sahara Desert, who have long revered it as a sacred site and a prominent feature in local folklore and traditions.

In recent years, expeditions to study the geological features and biodiversity of the Richat Structure have led to new discoveries, such as plant and animal species that have uniquely adapted to the harsh desert environment around it. But despite its remote location, the Richat Structure faces threats from human activities like mining, tourism, and climate change. Efforts are being made to protect and preserve its ecological and cultural significance for many more generations to come.

023. The Lost Cities of Sodom and Gomorrah

Divine intervention can be truly destructive, if the stories are anything to go by. But could these two cities have existed and been struck down in reality?

The story of Sodom and its sister city Gomorrah is recounted in the book of Genesis in the Bible, where they are described as cities of sin and vice. According to the scripture, these wicked cities were destroyed by divine fire and brimstone as a punishment for their immorality, leaving behind nothing but pillars of salt, ashes, and ruins.

The search for the real-life location of the two cities (Sodom, in particular) has long intrigued scholars and explorers. In recent decades, they have turned their attention to Tell el-Hammam, a sprawling archaeological site located in the Jordan Valley, northeast of the Dead Sea. Here, many believe they may have uncovered the remains of the ancient city of Sodom.

Excavations at Tell el-Hammam have revealed a fortified city dating back over 4,000 years, which lines up with the time period when Sodom is believed to have been in its prime. The site features massive defensive walls and evidence of urban planning, which suggest that it was once a thriving city.

One of the most intriguing discoveries at Tell el-Hammam is a layer of ash and debris dating to the Late Bronze Age, around 1650 BCE. This layer aligns with the biblical timeframe for the destruction of Sodom and Gomorrah, which has led some researchers to consider that the ruins at Tell el-Hammam may indeed be ancient Sodom.

Geological evidence of seismic activity and the presence of sulfur deposits in the area provide more proof of the city's fiery demise. However, evidence has also been marred by false claims and altered photographic evidence, which has led many to remain skeptical. In addition, there are still many inconsistencies with the biblical narrative and the remains found at the site, as well as alternative theories about the city's location. The debate around this site continues to fuel scholarly inquiry and exploration.

024. The 24 Stone Coffins of Saqqara

In 1850, French archaeologist Auguste Mariette unearthed a remarkable discovery near the Step Pyramid of Djoser in Saqqara, Egypt. Hidden beneath the desert sands lay the first clues to a burial place that contained 24 ancient sarcophagi, or stone coffins, dating back over 2,500 years to the Late Period of ancient Egyptian history.

What makes these stone coffins so intriguing is their exquisite craftsmanship. Carved from solid blocks of "costly stone" like granite and basalt (as opposed to the more typically used limestone), each coffin is decorated with hieroglyphic inscriptions, vibrant colors, and intricate artwork. The precision and skill exhibited in the construction of these stone coffins are remarkable. From the perfectly smoothed surfaces to the fine detail in the carvings, every aspect of the coffins demonstrates a mastery of stone carving techniques, the likes of which can only be achieved today with modern laser technology!

Notably though, while similar sarcophagi were commonly used to house the remains of high-ranking individuals, such as priests or officials, the 24 stone coffins in Saqqara were used for something quite different: bulls. More specifically, sacred bulls.

In Egyptian mythology, a key figure of worship was Apis, son of the goddess Hathor. Apis took the form of a bull, and represented strength, courage, and rebirth. As a result, the worship of Apis in certain cults was carried out through sacred bulls, who were chosen at birth, cared for by priests in their temples, and then sacrificed as part of the ritual worship of Apis. The bulls were then embalmed and ceremonially buried in sarcophagi together with valuables—much like how pharaohs were buried.

Despite the remarkable state in which they were found, the stone coffins face threats from modern-day environmental factors, such as pollution, humidity, and groundwater. Archaeologists and conservationists are currently working to ensure the long-term preservation of these invaluable artifacts.

025. The Bimini Road

The Bimini Road (also known as the Bimini Wall) was first discovered in 1968 by divers exploring the waters off the coast of North Bimini Island in the Bahamas close to Puerto Rico. Stretching for nearly half a mile along the ocean floor, this peculiar formation consists of a series of large, flat limestone blocks arranged in an eerily straight line.

Is it a man-made structure or a natural geological formation? This is one of the most hotly debated questions surrounding it. Some researchers argue that the alignment and symmetry of the limestone blocks suggest human intervention. Supporters of this idea speculate that it may be a remnant of an ancient civilization that existed thousands of years ago, like Atlantis!

Some theorists propose that the road may have been a part of a larger complex built by the Atlanteans in their capital city. Since the builders had advanced knowledge of engineering, they could easily have constructed the road to serve as a major route for navigation, or for ceremonial purposes.

On the other hand, skeptics argue that the Bimini Road is simply a natural formation caused by the weathering and erosion of limestone rock over a long period of time. As proof, they point to similar geological features found in other underwater parts of the world.

Over the years, scientists have conducted various studies and surveys of the Bimini Road to try to discover its origins. While some research shows the formation may have been altered by human activity, no conclusive evidence has been found yet of the structure's possibly artificial nature. The Bimini Road continues to captivate the imagination of adventurers and explorers worldwide and is one of countless mysteries that lie beneath the surface of our oceans.

026. The Olmec Colossal Heads

One of many civilizations that faded from history over time, the legacy of the Olmecs can be found in their colossal statues of heads. But why were they built?

The Olmec colossal heads are a collection of massive stone sculptures created by the ancient Olmec civilization, which flourished in what is now Mexico from around 1400 BCE to 400 BCE. The heads were first found in the 19th century, and have since become iconic symbols of Olmec culture. Seventeen of these heads have been found in the Olmec heartland, toward the south of the Gulf of Mexico.

The Olmec colossal heads are known for their impressive size and craftsmanship. Each of these monumental heads depicts a human face with distinct features: prominent lips, broad noses, and flattened heads. They were carved from basalt boulders that weighed from 6 to 50 tons!

The creation of the Olmec colossal heads is a feat of engineering and artistic skill. Scholars are still puzzled by how the Olmec, without the use of metal tools or even beasts of burden, were able to quarry, transport, and carve such massive stone statues with any kind of precision and accuracy. Some even suggest that the heads may have been moved over long distances using advanced engineering methods that have since been lost to history… or perhaps they had help from extraterrestrial beings.

The significance of the Olmec colossal heads is a subject of debate among archaeologists and historians. Some believe they represent powerful Olmec rulers or deities—each head has very distinctive headgear on them—while others speculate that they may have served as markers for important ritual or ceremonial sites. Some of the headgear on the heads has been linked to an ancient ball game the Olmecs played, suggesting the heads may have been important in Olmec sports culture.

After decades of study, many mysteries surrounding the Olmec colossal heads remain unsolved. But whether symbols of power, representations of gods, or markers of sacred sites, they continue to inspire awe in all those who gaze upon them.

027. The Nazca Lines

Created by the Nazca culture, which flourished in the region between 200 BCE and 600 CE, The Nazca Lines are hundreds of intricate drawings etched into the floor of the Nazca Desert in southern Peru. Although thousands of years have passed since their creation, the clarity of the lines has been well preserved due to the dry climate and lack of plant life in the Nazca Desert.

Some of the designs include geometric shapes, animals, and humanoid figures, and all were done with remarkable precision. These are enormous as drawings go, with some spanning over 1,000 feet in length, so can only be fully appreciated when seen from the skies above, which has led to much speculation about why they were drawn in the first place.

The construction of the Nazca Lines required very thorough planning and accuracy, as the designs were created by removing the reddish-brown pebbles (which get their color from a coating of iron oxide) that cover the desert surface to reveal the lighter brown earth beneath. The Nazca people would have used simple tools, like sticks and stones, to mark the lines, which meant they would have relied on a fairly advanced understanding of geometry and surveying.

But *why* did these ancient people sketch diagrams in the desert that they themselves could not have seen in their full glory? Some believe they were used as pathways for ceremonies or rituals, while others have suggested they were a kind of star-based calendar or markers of underground water sources. It is also thought likely that they held a religious or spiritual significance for the Nazca people.

The Nazca lines were designated a UNESCO (United Nations Educational, Scientific and Cultural Organization) World Heritage Site in 1994. Centuries after they were engraved in the sands, these geoglyphs are a testament to the ingenuity of the Nazca civilization, and may yet offer greater insight into their beliefs, customs, and way of life.

028. The Holy Grail

So iconic that it is now a synonym for any goal that is elusive yet treasured, the Holy Grail is a legendary object said to possess miraculous powers, and is often linked to themes of redemption, spiritual enlightenment, and the quest for eternal life in medieval legends. It is also significant in Christian lore, as it is believed to be the cup used by Jesus Christ himself during the Last Supper.

The story and legacy of the Holy Grail have many ties to tales of King Arthur and his Knights of the Round Table. In Arthurian legend, the quest for the Holy Grail becomes the central focus of the knights' pursuits of chivalry, and is the key symbol of their quest for purity and spiritual fulfillment.

The quest for the Holy Grail has been depicted in countless literary works, poems, films, and video games, with each offering its own interpretation of the legendary tale. From Sir Galahad's noble quest for purity to the trials faced by Sir Percival and Sir Gawain, to the more modern search for it by famed fictional explorer Indiana Jones, the quest for the Grail is a timeless theme of heroism and self-discovery.

Legendary though it may be, the historical origins of the Holy Grail are shrouded in mystery. Some scholars believe the concept of the Grail may have been inspired by ancient Celtic or pagan myths, while others suggest it was originally one of the ancient relics or sacred vessels associated with early Christian rituals.

In fact, one of the biggest ongoing debates about the Holy Grail is whether it was even a physical artifact to begin with. Some scholars and theologians suggest that the actual purpose of the Holy Grail was to be a symbolic representation of spiritual truth. So while some believe that the Grail was a tangible object, others consider it simply a metaphor for divine grace and enlightenment.

Whether it was a symbol of divine grace or a tangible relic of ancient power, the legend of the Holy Grail continues to captivate the imaginations of people around the world. In modern times, the quest for the Holy Grail has taken on new meaning; it has been embraced by spiritual seekers, artists, and writers as a depiction of humanity's eternal search for truth, purpose, and transcendence from a world filled with challenges and uncertainties.

029. Lost Civilizations

Nothing beside remains. Round the decay of that colossal wreck, boundless and bare, the lone and level sands stretch far away. - "Ozymandias" by Percy Bysshe Shelley

One of the key messages of this famous poem about a great ruler named Ozymandias is that no matter how grand and far-reaching an empire may be, it will inevitably fall to the ravages of time. Many such civilizations have come and gone in the history of humanity; the few clues that remain of them today are a far cry from the glory of their prime.

Dating back to 3300 BCE, the Indus Valley Civilization flourished in what is now present-day Pakistan and northwest India. Known for its advanced urban planning, well-designed drainage systems, and sophisticated handicrafts and metalworking, the Indus Valley Civilization was one of the three great civilizations in its region, together with the Egyptians and the Mesopotamians.

Nestled in the desert landscapes of modern-day Jordan, the Nabataeans thrived from the 4th century BCE to the 1st century CE. They were renowned for their mastery of water conservation and their unique architecture cut out from rocks. They left behind a legacy of awe-inspiring monuments and marvels of engineering, including the legendary city of Petra.

On the island of Crete, the Minoan civilization emerged during the Bronze Age and reached its peak around 2000 BCE. They were known for their vibrant frescoes, elaborate palaces, and a maritime trade network that was advanced for its time. They also played a key role in the cultural landscape of the Aegean region, setting the stage for the ancient Greek civilization to come.

Located near present-day St. Louis, Missouri, Cahokia was the largest pre-Columbian settlement in North America, and the main city of the Mississippian culture, a Native American civilization that flourished in what is now the Midwestern, Eastern, and Southeastern United States from approximately 800 to 1600 CE. Cahokia was a complex society that thrived on trade and agriculture, existing between 1050 and 1350 CE. Today the Cahokia Mounds State Historic Site, one of 25 UNESCO World Heritage Sites in the US, consists of 80 enormous manmade mounds, the largest prehistoric earthen construction in the Americas north of Mexico.

Great Zimbabwe was an ancient city built by the Shona people in present-day Zimbabwe, and it flourished from the 11th to the 15th century CE. Great Zimbabwe was a center of wealth and power in southern Africa and was renowned for its intricate goldwork, extensive trade networks, and impressive stone architecture, such as the Zimbabwe birds, soapstone sculptures found in the ruins of the medieval city.

The Mayans were an advanced Mesoamerican civilization whose territory included present-day Mexico, Guatemala, Belize, Honduras, and El Salvador from around 2000 BCE to 900 CE. Known for their impressive pyramids, detailed calendar system, complex mathematics, and sophisticated writing system, the Mayans were among the most culturally rich and technologically advanced people of their time.

Despite all their achievements, the fates of these ancient civilizations remain a mystery. From natural disasters like climate change to invasions by foreign cultures, the factors that could have caused their decline and eventual disappearance continue to puzzle historians and archaeologists. Still, the legacies of these lost civilizations live on in their art, architecture, and cultural achievements, from the majestic ruins of Petra to the enigmatic pyramids of the Mayans.

CHAPTER 2: HISTORICAL MYSTERIES

030. The Mystery of the Mary Celeste

The story of the Mary Celeste begins in 1872, when the brigantine ship set sail in early November from New York City on a course to Genoa, Italy, carrying a cargo of alcohol. However, what was supposed to be a routine trading voyage would turn into one of the greatest maritime mysteries of all time.

Nearly a month after its departure, on December 4th, the Mary Celeste was found drifting aimlessly near the Azorean islands in the middle of the Atlantic Ocean by the crew of Canadian brigantine Dei Gratia. To the astonishment of the Dei Gratia's crew, the ship was completely deserted, with no sign of the captain, crew, or passengers!

Despite how eerie it appeared, the Mary Celeste showed no signs of distress, foul play, or any kind of trouble on board. Its cargo of alcohol and provisions were largely intact, and all the personal belongings of the missing crew had been left behind. The only clue to the crew's disappearance was a missing lifeboat and an absence of navigation equipment.

What could have caused the crew of the Mary Celeste to vanish without a trace? Speculation ranges from the more mundane possibilities (the ship fell victim to piracy, mutiny, or foul weather) to the fanciful: they could have been attacked by a giant sea creature, abducted by aliens, or tampered with by supernatural forces!

A salvage inquiry was conducted to figure out the cause of the crew's disappearance. An extensive investigation followed, but no conclusive evidence was found to explain the mystery. The crew of the Mary

Celeste were never found again, and their fate remains shrouded in uncertainty. As for the ship itself, it met a sad end in 1884, when a later captain wrecked her off the coast of Haiti in an insurance fraud scheme.

The mystery of the Mary Celeste has left its mark on popular culture, showing up in countless books, films, and TV shows about mysteriously abandoned ships. It is a tale that continues to fascinate people around the world, fueling fascination and intrigue about the dark secrets of the ocean.

031. The Disappearance of the Roanoke Colony

In the span of a few years, an entire settlement disappeared from sight. What happened to the people of Roanoke Colony?

In 1587, English colonists, led by John White, established a settlement on Roanoke Island off the coast of what is today North Carolina. The colony had been founded in 1585 by Governor Ralph Lane, but the first attempt at a settlement failed due to a lack of supplies and troubles with the local American Indian tribes. Two years later, John White was tasked with trying again, and the second attempt would be England's first permanent settlement in the New World. But fate had other ideas.

After leading the colonists to Roanaoke Island, White returned to England in 1588 to fetch more supplies, but the Anglo-Spanish War delayed his return until 1590. When he returned two years later, he found the entire colony had vanished! The only clues left behind were the enigmatic words "Croatoan" carved into a post and "Cro" etched into a tree. Before he could investigate further, though, his crew were forced to return to England due to lost equipment, and the roughly 120 colonists on Roanoke Island would never be found.

What happened to the Roanoke Colony? Some historians suggest they may have fallen victim to disease, famine, or conflict with American

Indian tribes in the area, as Governor Lane's colony had done before them. Others have proposed more outlandish explanations, from abduction by aliens to a secret integration into neighboring American Indian communities.

This last theory has some basis in the clues that were left behind; the "Croatoan" carving could have referred to the nearby Croatoan tribe, whom the colonists could have settled with. Artifacts and DNA analysis have also recently provided some evidence for this theory, though none of it is conclusive.

And so the fate of the Lost Colony of Roanoke remains unresolved after centuries of investigation. While archaeologists continue to search for answers, the Lost Colony has left its mark on American history and culture. It has been the subject of countless books, films, and TV shows for all those fascinated with the unexplained.

032. The Lost City of Z

Many adventurers have risked their lives and braved the unknown to answer one question: is there a city of riches hidden in the jungles of the Amazon?

The legend of the Lost City of Z is often linked with the quest for El Dorado, another fabled city of untold treasures said to be hidden somewhere in the depths of the Amazon rainforest. Such hidden riches have been the dream find of various explorers and fortune seekers for centuries.

The Lost City of Z's story begins with British explorer Colonel Percy Fawcett, a man who had a reputation for surviving in extreme and hostile conditions in the jungle for years at a time. In 1925, Fawcett set out on an expedition to find the lost city, as he was convinced it existed based on indigenous legends and his own research.

But Fawcett and the two others in his expedition team vanished without a trace in the unforgiving wilderness of the Amazon in the Mato Grosso region of Brazil. Despite numerous search efforts over the years, their fate remains a mystery to this day, partly because Fawcett kept his route a secret, for fear that other explorers would find the Lost City of Z before him. This made it impossible for rescuers to retrace his steps.

As for the city itself, indigenous Amazonian tribes have long spoken of ancient cities hidden deep within the rainforest. In the years following Fawcett's disappearance, more expeditions were launched in search of the Lost City of Z. While some explorers claimed to have found evidence of ancient settlements, none were able to find the legendary city.

Recent archaeological discoveries in the Amazon have shed new light on the region's ancient civilizations. Advances in technology, such as Lidar mapping, have helped researchers penetrate the dense jungle canopy and uncover hidden ruins, which may lead to uncovering lost cities like Z, if they do indeed exist. But whether myth or reality, the quest for the Lost City of Z continues to draw adventurers and explorers into the uncharted depths of the Amazon in search of answers.

033. Jack the Ripper

In the autumn of 1888, London's East End was gripped by terror as a string of gruesome murders took place in Whitechapel, a district marked by extreme poverty and terrible living conditions. The victims, all women working as prostitutes, were mutilated and left for dead. This sparked a citywide manhunt for the elusive killer who came to be known as Jack the Ripper.

The culprit is believed to have claimed the lives of five victims: Mary Ann Nichols, Annie Chapman, Elizabeth Stride, Catherine Eddowes, and Mary Jane Kelly. Each murder had the hallmarks of a savage yet methodical killer, and sent ripples of fear and paranoia through the streets of Victorian London.

During the height of the Whitechapel murders, a series of taunting letters were sent to the police at Scotland Yard, as well as to local newspapers, apparently from the killer himself. These infamous "Ripper letters" added even more intrigue to the mystery of the identity of Jack the Ripper.

But although exhaustive investigations were carried out by Scotland Yard and countless theories were put forward by historians and armchair detectives, the true identity of Jack the Ripper was never discovered. Over the years, numerous suspects have been suggested, ranging from doctors to aristocrats to artists—and even members of the royal family.

The study of Jack the Ripper and the Whitechapel murders has given rise to a dedicated group of enthusiasts known as Ripperologists. These amateur sleuths and historians devote countless hours to researching and analyzing the case even today, hoping to uncover the identity of the infamous murderer.

Advancements in forensic science have also led to renewed interest in the case. In recent years, researchers have used DNA analysis and other modern techniques to re-examine the evidence from the crime scenes, hoping to shed new light on the investigation and potential suspects.

In popular culture, the mystery of Jack the Ripper continues to captivate the public imagination and has spawned countless books, films, and TV shows. From an appearance in Arthur Conan Doyle's Sherlock Holmes series to more modern crime dramas and serial killer shows, the legend of Jack the Ripper lives on as a haunting reminder of the dark side of human nature and the longlasting appeal of unsolved mysteries.

034. The Princes in The Tower

This story begins with two young princes, Edward V and his brother, Richard of Shrewsbury, Duke of York, who were the sons of King Edward IV of England. Following their father's death in 1483, the princes (12 and 9 years old at the time) were lodged in the Tower of London by their uncle, Richard, Duke of Gloucester, who had been appointed their protector.

In a shocking turn of events, the Duke then declared the princes illegitimate, and seized the throne for himself, claiming the crown as King Richard III. Last seen inside the tower, no trace of either prince was ever found after the Duke seized power.

The disappearance of the young princes from the Tower of London has puzzled historians and sparked countless theories over the centuries. Some believe they were murdered on the orders of their uncle, who saw them as threats to his reign. However, although King Richard III has long been the primary suspect in their disappearance, given his motive to eliminate potential rivals to the throne and the opportunity to do so as their appointed protector, conclusive evidence of his guilt has never been found.

Some have suggested that Henry VII, who defeated Richard III at the Battle of Bosworth Field, may have been responsible, while others speculate that the princes may have been smuggled out of the tower by a third party with unknown motives. They may have wanted to protect the boys from Richard III's schemes, or to accelerate his ascendance to the throne.

Whatever the true circumstances, the fate of the Princes in the Tower continues to confound historians and enthusiasts alike.

035. The Piri Reis Map

In 1513, a skilled Ottoman admiral and cartographer, Piri Reis (Reis was a military rank equivalent to captain, so the name Piri Reis translates to Captain Piri), created a world map that would later become known as the Piri Reis Map, using a combination of his own surveys and older sources to put together a comprehensive depiction of the known world.

What sets the Piri Reis Map apart is how accurate and detailed it is, particularly in how it portrays the coastlines of Europe, Africa, and the Americas. For its time, the level of geographical knowledge that was displayed on the map was truly remarkable and ahead of other maps crafted during the same time period. It even included a depiction of Antarctica, a continent that wasn't officially discovered until centuries later!

The fact that the map shows a surprisingly accurate representation of the coastline of Antarctica has led to much debate about how Piri Reis could have known about it, which in turn has sparked discussion about how he drew up the map in the first place.

Some suggest that Piri may have used ancient maps or knowledge passed down through generations from mysterious origins. Others think the depiction of Antarctica could be a lucky guess, or the result of accidental discovery. Some of the more controversial claims contend that the map's accuracy is proof of advanced ancient civilizations or lost knowledge (whose maps Piri somehow got his hands on), but most dismiss such claims as unfounded and fanciful stories.

In recent years, radiocarbon dating of the parchment has confirmed its age, while studies using infrared imaging have revealed hidden details and even corrections made by Piri Reis himself while creating the map. But despite centuries of study and analysis, the truth behind the origins and construction process of the Piri Reis Map, as well as the secret of its remarkable accuracy, remain a mystery.

036. The Green Children of Woolpit

Fantasy realms with strange beings can be found very easily in fairy tales. But is it possible they exist in the real world too?

During the 12th century, the village of Woolpit in England was the site of a strange, almost paranormal event. According to historical accounts, villagers stumbled upon two children, a brother and sister, wandering near the mouth of a wolf pit, which is how the village got the name 'Woolpit'. These two children stood out because they spoke an unfamiliar language, and their skin was a peculiar shade of green!

The children's clothing was also of an unusual fabric, and they would only eat raw broad beans. But in spite of their mysterious origins, the villagers of Woolpit took in the green children and cared for them. Over time, the siblings lost the green in their skin color and learned to eat other food. While the boy died young, the girl grew up to be rebellious and carefree. She even learned to speak English, and told the villagers that she and her brother had come from a place called Saint Martin's Land, where the sun never shone and everything was green.

The origins of the green children of Woolpit have puzzled historians and scholars for centuries, especially because Saint Martin's Land has never been found. Some suggest that they may have come from a subterranean world or an alternate dimension, while others propose more realistic explanations: for example, one hypothesis suggests that the green children may have been Flemish immigrants who became lost or orphaned. Or they may have been survivors of a famine or plague, which could explain their disoriented state.

The tale of the green children of Woolpit has inspired folklore and fascination for centuries, as well as countless retellings and interpretations, but its true origins remain a mystery. Were they visitors from another world or victims of circumstance? Perhaps one day the answer will be found by future scholars.

037. The Man in the Iron Mask

Many of us have heard of the Man in the Iron Mask, at least from movies and popular culture references, but the real-life story begins in the late 17th century, during the reign of King Louis XIV of France.

According to historical accounts, a mysterious prisoner given the pseudonym of "Eustache Dauger" had his identity concealed by a mask made of iron, and was imprisoned in various French jails for over three decades.

He was held in the custody of the French state, and always guarded closely by a select group of trusted officials. But although he was a prisoner, he was also treated with an unusual degree of respect and dignity, leading to speculation about who he truly was.

Over the years, many theories have been proposed about the identity of the Man in the Iron Mask. Some suggest he may have been a high-ranking nobleman, a political rival, or even a secret twin brother of King Louis XIV himself.

In line with this latter idea, one popular theory claims that the man was a close relative of the king, such as a sibling or illegitimate son, whose existence was a threat to the stability of the monarchy. To protect the royal lineage and maintain political power, the king imprisoned him and had his identity hidden from the public with the infamous mask of iron.

The mystery of the Man in the Iron Mask has inspired countless works of literature. His most famous appearance is likely in the Alexandre Dumas novel *The Vicomte of Bragelonne: Ten Years Later*, in which the character is revealed to be the twin brother of King Louis XIV. But while the story has captured the imagination of writers and filmmakers, historians continue to debate its accuracy. Some believe that the tale may have been embellished or distorted over time, and that there never truly was a man in an iron mask to begin with! Others suggest that there is a grain of truth to the legend, although what that truth might be is a matter of debate.

Whether fact or fiction, the Man in the Iron Mask remains one of history's greatest enigmas, and offers a fascinating look at the intrigue and secrecy that surrounded the royal courts of Europe in the 17th century.

038. The Dancing Plague of 1518

In July 1518, a woman named Frau Troffea stepped into the streets of Strasbourg (modern-day France) and began to dance, much like how one might begin a flash mob today. But this was no ordinary dance. Frau Troffea moved fervently and recklessly without stopping for nearly a week!

While she was in her trance-like frenzy, a few dozen others joined in. The desire to dance spread like a plague throughout the city, causing somewhere from 50 to 400 people to give in to the urge to dance day and night, often until they collapsed from exhaustion or were badly injured.

Although local authorities and doctors tried to stop them, the craze lasted well into September, even taking the lives of some while leaving others in a state of physical and mental distress. Medical scholars at the time were utterly baffled by the phenomenon, unable to either diagnose or treat the mysterious affliction.

What happened to the people of Strasbourg in 1518? Some historians and scholars think that the dancing plague may have been caused by mass hysteria, psychological stress, or even religious passion, especially since the strange event took place during a time when major issues such as famine, disease, and religious turmoil were widespread in Europe. These factors could have led to the outbreak, as people may have initially wanted to find some relief from their troubles through communal dancing. Others have suggested more unusual explanations, like mass food poisoning or even demonic possession!

The dancing plague of 1518 is one of history's cautionary tales about the power of mass hysteria and the mysteries of the human mind. Artists, writers, and scholars have explored its meaning and significance over the centuries, sparking debate about the unpredictable nature of human behavior.

039. The Lost Ship of the Colorado Desert

When ships go missing, they can be expected to be found drifting in the ocean, or washed up on shore. How does a ship end up in the middle of an arid desert though?

The first account of a treasure ship in the Colorado Desert comes from the mid-19th century, when explorer Colonel Albert S. Evans reported coming across a half-buried ship in a drying-up salt lake near Dos Palmas in California. However, when other expeditions set out to find the ship, it seemed to have vanished... or perhaps it had never been there.

Other accounts of a stranded ship in the Colorado Desert have emerged over the years since. A prospector in the 1930s reported seeing a ship lodged inside the rock of Canebrake Canyon in southern California. An earthquake struck the area shortly afterward, though, making his trail to the ship impossible to follow, and possibly burying the ship in the process as well.

As the legend of the Lost Ship of the Colorado Desert spread, so too did rumors of its contents. Some suggested that it had been carrying a cargo of gold, while others link the ship to a pearl-harvesting expedition carried out by Spanish explorer Juan de Iturbe in the early 17th century, whose ship was said to hold a fortune in black pearls before it ran aground near the Gulf of California.

One of the biggest questions about the Lost Ship is what kind of ship it was. Colonel Evans described it to look like a Spanish galleon in design, but other accounts describe the ship as having the long neck and round metal shields of a Viking ship. How a ship from the ancient Norse seafarers could have wound up near California is a mystery that defies explanation though!

Whatever its origins may be, and wherever the ship may actually be located within the vast expanse of the Colorado Desert, the Lost Ship continues to be sought after by adventurers and treasure hunters even today.

040. The Amber Room

The Amber Room was a chamber in the Catherine Palace in Tsarskoye Selo, near Saint Petersburg in Russia. Originally created in the 18th century, it was masterpiece of workmanship and opulence. Crafted from over six tons of amber, gold leaf, and precious gemstones, it was considered one of the wonders of the world.

The Amber Room was initially intended for King Frederick I of Prussia, and was installed in Berlin City Palace. But when Peter the Great of Russia admired it during a visit in 1716, King Frederick's son, Frederick William I, presented the room to Peter as a gift, which forged a Russo-Prussian alliance. Covering more than 590 square feet, its ornate designs made it a prized possession of the Russian royal family for over two centuries.

Sadly, during World War II, when German forces invaded the Soviet Union in 1941, the Nazis looted the Catherine Palace and dismantled the Amber Room, intending to transport it to Germany as spoils of war. But then at some point in the chaos of war, the precious panels and treasures somehow vanished without a trace.

The disappearance of the Amber Room has led to much scholarly debate over the years following the end of the war. Some believe it was destroyed during bombing raids or lost at sea during transport, while others suggest that it was hidden away in a secret location by the Nazis, the details of which were lost in the midst of their defeat.

In the decades since, numerous expeditions and searches have been launched in an attempt to find out what happened to the Amber Room. But despite some tantalizing leads and even apparent sightings, no conclusive evidence of where it ended up has ever been found. A reconstruction of the Amber Room at the Catherine Palace was begun in 1979 and completed in 2003, although whether it captures the grandeur of the original will never be known.

041. The Tomb of Genghis Khan

Genghis Khan, born Temüjin in 1162, was the eldest son of a Mongol clan leader. When he was eight, his father died and his family was abandoned by the clan. But from these humble beginnings, he grew up to become the founder and first khan of the Mongol Empire, the largest empire in history over a single land mass. Adopting the title "Genghis Khan" at an assembly in 1206, he is known for his military genius and ruthless leadership, and had a powerful impact on world history.

Legends say that the great Khan was buried with untold riches and treasures to match his status as a conqueror, which made his tomb a tantalizing prize for treasure hunters and scholars alike. But according to a tale by famous explorer Marco Polo, the 2000 slaves who buried Khan's remains and carried out his funeral were then executed by the soldiers who had guarded them. These soldiers were in turn killed by loyal assassins who then committed suicide, ensuring that no one who knew the location of the tomb was left alive!

For centuries, archaeologists have tried and failed to find the whereabouts of Khan's final resting place. While various likely places have been suggested as possible burial sites, such as the sacred mountain of Burkhan Khaldun in Mongolia, no definitive evidence has been found to confirm the location of the tomb.

Folklore and legends in Mongolia are rich with stories about the tomb, and many local communities there claim to be descended from the custodians of his burial site. Historical records from Khan's time, like those of Marco Polo, offer vague clues but nothing more.

In recent years, modern technology and archaeological techniques like ground-penetrating radar, satellite imaging, and drones have been used to survey potential burial sites, but so far, the tomb's location has remained a mystery. Wherever it might be hidden under the vast expanse of the Mongolian steppes, the tomb of the Great Genghis Khan will forever beckon to adventurers and historians determined to uncover such a compelling mystery.

042. El Dorado

The invaders and adventurers of South America were drawn to it like flies to honey—but what is the truth behind the gold of El Dorado?

El Dorado, "The Golden One" in Spanish, is a mythical place said to be located somewhere in the unexplored wilds of South America.

According to the legends, it was said to be filled to the brim with gold and precious jewels, drawing treasure hunters from far and wide like moths to a flame. What exactly El Dorado was is also unclear, with conflicting accounts describing it as anything from a single city to a grand empire.

The quest for El Dorado began in the 16th century, when Spanish conquistadors first travelled to the New World in search of gold and glory. Driven by tales of the rich offerings from some of the native tribes, expeditions were launched to uncover the elusive city of gold that was rumored to be the source of their riches, and this led to centuries of exploration and speculation.

One of the most well-known legends of El Dorado was a coronation ritual performed by the Muisca people who lived in present-day Colombia. During this ceremony, the newly appointed tribal chief would cover himself in gold dust and head out in a raft laden with gold, emeralds, and other riches to the center of the sacred lake Guatavita, where the offerings would be thrown into the lake as a symbol of the chief's divine connection to the earth and the gods. The chief was called *El Rey Dorado,* or "The Golden King," and it is thought that the legend of El Dorado has its origins in this ceremony.

But after many years and countless failed expeditions, the fabled city of El Dorado remains out of reach. Many adventurers have lost their lives in the pursuit of this mythical place, and others only had tales of hardship and disappointment to show for their efforts. So, did El Dorado truly exist, or was it simply a figment of the imagination and an ideal subject for native storytellers?

While most people today have come to think of it as a myth, some believe that the city or kingdom may still be hidden deep inside the uncharted jungles of the Amazon basin, waiting to be discovered by anyone brave or determined enough to seek it out. Whatever the truth, the legend of El Dorado as a city of gold forever lost to time remains one of history's greatest mysteries and has been the subject of countless songs, books, films, and video games through the ages.

043. The MV Joyita Ghost Ship

The MV Joyita was an American merchant vessel that sailed the waters of the South Pacific Ocean in the mid-20th century. First built in 1931 as a luxury yacht for movie director Roland West, who named the ship *Joyita,* "Little Jewel" in Spanish, after his wife, this 69-foot wooden ship was used for various purposes by different owners over its years of service, one of which was as a trade and charter boat between Pacific islands.

In October 1955, the MV Joyita set off on a routine voyage from Samoa to the Tokelau Islands, carrying passengers and cargo as usual. However, the ship failed to arrive at its destination. Although it had not sent out a distress signal, authorities launched a massive search and rescue operation to find the missing vessel.

Nearly a month later, they found the MV Joyita adrift in the open ocean, hundreds of miles off course from its route. To the shock of its rescuers, it was not only deserted, but also damaged to the point of sinking. The ship was partially submerged and tilted to its port side, and was missing all of its lifeboats and equipment, as well as four tons of cargo.

The discovery of the deserted ship sparked a frenzy of speculation: what had happened to the passengers and crew? Why did they abandon the ship? And why was it found in such poor condition?

Some theories suggested that the ship may have been attacked by pirates or leftover Japanese fighters from the recently ended World War II, while others postulated that the crew could have been injured and unable to operate the ship any longer. Another theory was that some kind of insurance fraud or mutiny was involved. But after many thorough investigations by maritime authorities, the true fate of the MV Joyita's crew remains unknown.

044. The Miracle of the Sun

The Miracle of the Sun is a series of events that occurred on October 13, 1917, near the village of Fátima in Portugal. Large crowds gathered in Fátima after hearing of prophecies from three shepherd children: Lucia dos Santos and her cousins, Francisco and Jacinta Marto.

Months before the Miracle of the Sun, the children claimed that the Virgin Mary (whom they called Our Lady of Fátima) had appeared to them and left them with divine wisdom, including predictions of the end of World War I and the rise of communism, and the need for repentance and faith from the people of Portugal. They said that on the 13th of October, the Virgin Mary would appear and perform miracles to prove her identity.

On the day of the miracle, an estimated 70,000 people gathered at Cova da Iria, a quarter in the city of Fátima, hoping to witness the promised divine acts of God for themselves. As the crowd looked to the sky, they witnessed the sun dance, spin, and emit vivid colors, casting multicolored rays of light across the sky! Some observers even claimed to have seen the sun appear to plunge toward the Earth before returning to its normal position.

Following the Miracle of the Sun, many of those present reported experiencing a profound spiritual awakening. The event also gave Fátima its reputation as a sacred pilgrimage site for Catholics around the world.

While the Miracle of the Sun has been embraced by many as divine intervention, skeptics have offered many alternative explanations, from mass hallucination to optical illusions caused by strange atmospheric conditions. The explanations have so far failed to fully account for the sheer scale and complexity of the reported sightings, though. Whatever its origins may be, the Miracle of the Sun remains one of the most extraordinary events in modern religious history.

045. The Oak Island Money Pit

The story of the Oak Island Money Pit dates back to 1795, when a young boy named Daniel McGinnis stumbled upon a peculiar depression in the ground on Oak Island in Nova Scotia, Canada. Intrigued by the prospect of buried treasure, McGinnis and his friends began to explore the site. They became the first of many such treasure hunters.

McGinnis and his companions dug deeper into the ground, finding layers of logs and debris every ten feet, so they believed they had stumbled upon a buried treasure vault. But as they continued to dig, the pit became flooded with seawater, forcing them to abandon their search.

Over the years, many other attempts have been made to excavate the Money Pit, with various methods used to bypass the flooded tunnels and reach the alleged treasure chamber, from elaborate drilling operations to sonar imaging. No expense has been spared in the quest to unlock the secrets of Oak Island. But the Oak Island Money Pit is also rumored to be cursed, as many tragedies and accidents have befallen those who dared to seek its treasure.

What could be hidden inside the Oak Island Money Pit? Some believe it may be the hiding place of treasure collected by the famed pirate Captain Kidd, while others think it could contain lost relics like the Holy Grail or the Ark of the Covenant, or even evidence of extraterrestrial visits!

In recent years, the search for answers on Oak Island has progressed with the help of advances in archaeological techniques. Ground-penetrating radar, high-tech pumps and underwater drones have been used to survey the island and uncover clues about its mysterious past. Markings and pieces found at the site have links to ancient societies like the Freemasons and Rosicrucians. But the treasure, if there is one, has yet to be found.

046. The Loretto Chapel Staircase

The Loretto Chapel, located in Santa Fe, New Mexico, is known for its stunning Gothic architecture. Built in the late 19th century, the chapel's most notable feature is its miraculous staircase, which seems to defy the laws of physics with its unique design and construction.

The Loretto Chapel staircase is a spiral that rises 20 feet high and features two complete 360-degree turns along the way with no visible means of support. It is constructed entirely of wood, with no nails or glue holding it together. Handrails were added later, when the nuns found it so unnerving to descend the spiral that they did so on all fours. More than a hundred experts have analyzed the staircase, but none have figured out how it was constructed!

According to legend, the chapel's original architect died before completing the staircase, leaving the nuns with no way to access the choir loft. In their desperation, the nuns prayed to St. Joseph, the patron saint of carpenters, and a mysterious stranger then came to them, offering to build the staircase that would solve their problem.

The stranger, who some believe to have been St. Joseph himself, worked in secret and used only simple tools, with no scaffolding or other support system. When the intricate staircase was completed, the stranger simply vanished without collecting his pay or revealing his identity!

Who was the mysterious carpenter? Those who don't accept that it was divine intervention suggest that it may have been a French rancher named Frank Rochas, who had moved to New Mexico around that time and was known to be an expert craftsman, although there is no solid evidence that he wa the one who built the staircase.

The Loretto Chapel staircase continues to this day to captivate pilgrims, tourists, and architectural enthusiasts from around the world.

047. The Codex Gigas

Could the Devil have had a hand in the writing of the Codex Gigas?

The Codex Gigas is a medieval manuscript believed to have been created in the early 13th century. It measures 36 inches tall, 20 inches wide, and 9 inches thick, making it one of the largest medieval manuscripts to have survived to this day.

Legend has it that the Codex Gigas was the work of a single monk who made a pact with the Devil to complete the manuscript in a single night. According to the tale, the monk was to be executed by his order for breaking his monastic vows, and promised to create a book containing all the knowledge of humanity in exchange for his life. To fulfill his end of the bargain, he called upon the Devil's aid, and the result was the creation of the Codex Gigas.

The book contains a diverse range of texts that include the complete Vulgate (late-4th-century Latin translation of the Bible), historical records, texts about medicine, and various other works. Its most famous feature is a large, full-page illustration of Satan, which has strengthened its associations with the Devil in the manuscript's origin story.

The Codex Gigas also contains other intricate drawings and decorations, including artwork of heavenly scenes, architectural designs, and even some fairly elaborate calligraphy. Its contents provide many insights into the scholarly and spiritual world of the Middle Ages.

Today, the Codex Gigas is housed in the National Library of Sweden in Stockholm, where it is carefully preserved and protected. The manuscript itself is not typically on public display due to its fragility, but high-resolution digital images of its pages are available for scholars and enthusiasts to study. There are many unanswered questions about the book: Who was the mysterious monk who created it? What inspired the devilish legend of its creation? And are there more secrets remaining within its pages?

048. The Fate of the Knights Templar

The Knights Templar was founded in the early 12th century CE as a military order that protected Christian pilgrims traveling to the Holy Land during the Crusades. They began as only nine knights, but the order quickly grew in influence to become one of the most powerful organizations in Europe. Some have said they were one of the earliest prototypes of a multinational corporation!

The Knights Templar gathered a large amount of wealth and property, and held vast estates, castles, and treasures throughout Europe and the Middle East. Legend has it that some of the treasures collected during their time in the Holy Land include the Holy Grail and the Ark of the Covenant from the Temple Mount in Jerusalem. Many of the tales claim that the spiritual powers in these artifacts were what helped them to become so powerful.

But in the early 14th century CE, the Templars fell out of favor with the church and European royalty. They were accused of heresy, blasphemy, corruption, financial fraud, and conducting secret rituals, which led to their persecution by King Philip IV of France and Pope Clement V.

On October 13, 1307, King Philip IV ordered the arrest of hundreds of Templars, many of whom were tortured and forced to confess to their crimes, while others were executed. The events of that day became known as the Friday the 13th Massacre, and marked the beginning of the end for the Templars.

Oddly enough, no one knows for certain what happened to the Templars after that day. Some believe the order was completely broken up, and all of its members executed or imprisoned, while others believe the Templars went underground and continued to operate in secret. Many of the treasures they possessed were never recovered either, which only added to the mystery of their fate.

Whatever became of them in the end, the legacy of the Knights Templar lives on in pop culture today, as references to the Templars both past and possibly present can be found in many books, films, and video games.

CHAPTER 3: MODERN MYSTERIES

049. The Bermuda Triangle

The Bermuda Triangle, also known as the Devil's Triangle, is a loosely defined region in the western part of the North Atlantic Ocean. The three points of the triangle are the southern tip of Florida and the islands of Bermuda and Puerto Rico. Stretching over approximately 500,000 square miles, ships and aircraft have mysteriously vanished over the years while traveling through this area. At least 20 confirmed disappearances have been reported, and the number of missing people is well into the hundreds.

The legend of the Bermuda Triangle dates back to the early 19th century, when the schooner *USS Pickering* went missing on a voyage from Guadeloupe to Delaware with more than 90 people on board. One of the more famous incidents occurred in 1945 when Flight 19, a squadron of five US Navy bombers, all disappeared in the area during a training exercise. Despite extensive search efforts, none of the planes were ever found.

The theories that have been proposed to explain the mystery of the Bermuda Triangle range from the scientific to the paranormal: while some think the disappearances are caused by anomalies in the Earth's magnetic field or underwater methane gas eruptions, some of the more outlandish beliefs suggest the Triangle is the site of alien abductions or time fractures!

Many scientists and researchers believe that the incidents in the Bermuda Triangle are caused by natural events, such as unpredictable changes in weather, strong ocean currents, and sudden storms. These environmental factors, when combined with the vastness of the ocean, can create dangerous travel conditions for both ships and aircraft.

Another possible explanation for the disappearances is human error. Mistakes in navigation, mechanical failures, and bad decisions made by pilots and sailors can all lead to accidents and being lost at sea. The fact that these all occurred within the same region could be a coincidence, though a strange one.

The Bermuda Triangle has captured the imagination of writers, filmmakers, and conspiracy theorists for decades, and led to a plethora of books, movies, and documentaries. Its reputation of mystery and danger has become a fixture in popular culture, feeding the many myths and legends about its supposed supernatural powers.

Though the Bermuda Triangle is thought by many to be a mystical region, scientists are determined to study it using modern technology, like satellite imaging and underwater drones. This has enabled them to explore the ocean floor for clues about the disappearances, and they've actually found some of the wrecks from the doomed voyages. But others remain unsolved, and probably always will.

050. The Zodiac Killer

With every kill and every coded letter, the Zodiac Killer's infamy only grew more and more fearsome. But who was the man behind the vicious puzzle?

The Zodiac Killer was named for the chilling letters he sent to newspapers and law enforcement, and is believed to be responsible for a string of murders in Northern California between 1968 and 1974. His victims varied in age and gender, and he killed indiscriminately, instilling fear and panic in San Francisco's Bay Area. In his final letter, he claimed to have murdered 37 victims in total, but some estimates say it could have been even more!

One of the most perplexing aspects of the Zodiac Killer case is the series of cryptic codes and ciphers he included in some of his letters. They often began with the phrase, "This is the Zodiac speaking." His messages contained taunts, threats, and bizarre symbols, and of the four ciphers he sent, only two have been solved to date.

Despite many investigations and intensive manhunts by the San Francisco Police Department, the Zodiac Killer was never caught, and his identity and motives remain unknown. It is still one of the most infamous unsolved serial killer cases in history. While numerous suspects have been investigated over the years, none of them were proven to be the Zodiac Killer beyond any doubt, and many of them are now dead, though the case itself remains alive.

Witnesses who survived their encounters with the Zodiac Killer gave information to law enforcement to create composite sketches, but these images only added to the confusion about the killer's identity, because he wore a hood or mask during his attacks, which obscured his features. As for possible motives, some believe he was a loner with a grudge against society, while others think he may have even had ties with law enforcement or the military.

The Zodiac Killer case has had a lasting impact on popular culture, with a host of books, movies, and TV shows that have delved into the hunt for the killer. His cryptic messages and brazen attacks continue to fascinate and terrify audiences to this day, and his haunting legacy is a trail of unanswered questions and unsolved ciphers.

051. The Georgia Guidestones

Sometimes called the American version of Stonehenge, the Georgia Guidestones have prompted their own share of rumors.

The Georgia Guidestones was a granite monument erected on a hilltop in Elbert County, Georgia on March 22, 1980. Its sudden appearance sparked controversy about its origins and purpose, and the true identity of the person behind the monument's construction was never found.

The Guidestones consisted of four massive granite slabs arranged in a paddlewheel formation, together with a central granite pillar and a granite capstone. The four slabs stood over 19 feet tall, and the monument as a whole weighed more than 237,000 pounds.

Each slab was inscribed with a series of ten guidelines, or principles, written in eight different languages that included the seven most spoken languages in the world: English, Spanish, Swahili, Hindi, Hebrew, Arabic, Chinese, and Russian. The messages outlined ten principles for humanity to live by, and covered topics such as population control, caring for the environment, and the pursuit of knowledge, and were written as though to guide future generations toward a more peaceful and sustainable existence.

The monument's creator, identified only by the psuedonym "Robert C. Christian," commissioned its construction through a series of intermediaries, and left behind very few clues to his identity or motives. Decades after the Georgia Guidestones were erected, investigations still have not uncovered who the man truly was, or even if it was a single person or a group.

While some saw the Georgia Guidestones as a benevolent guide, others viewed it as an omen of a catastrophic future. Many conspiracy theories linked the monument to secret societies, government agendas, and even satanic rituals! The Georgia Guidestones were the target of vandalism and defacement over the years, until a bombing from an unknown vandal damaged the structure beyond repair on July 6, 2022, and the remains were moved to a third-party location for safety reasons. Whether they will be rebuilt again someday is one more unanswered question in this mystery.

052. The Dyatlov Pass Incident

In January 1959, a group of ten hikers from the Ural Polytechnic Institute in Russia, led by student Igor Dyatlov, embarked on an ambitious trek through the Ural Mountains. Their goal was to reach Otorten, a mountain in the northern Urals, but they never reached their destination.

Weeks after they left, search parties discovered the hikers' abandoned tent on the slopes of Kholat Syakhl, which is now known as Dyatlov Pass in memory of the hiking party. Inside the tent, investigators found signs of a hasty departure, with gear and belongings left behind. The bodies of the hikers themselves were found scattered in the surrounding area, some with signs of severe trauma.

The cause of death for the hikers was determined to be hypothermia due to a lack of proper clothing, but the circumstances surrounding their demise raised more questions than answers. Some of the bodies showed strange physical injuries, such as fractured skulls and bruising consistent with high-impact forces.

The cause of the Dyatlov Pass Incident has baffled investigators for decades. The most popular theory is that they were struck by an avalanche, but it does not account for all the clues found at the site. Could it have been an animal attack, a harsh snowstorm—or something more sinister? The lack of conclusive evidence has led to all manner of conspiracy theories. There are some who think it was a government cover-up, while others speculate that the group came across clandestine military experiments or even extraterrestrial beings!

The Soviet authorities launched two official investigations into the incident, the most recent of which was in 2019 and concluded that the cause of the hikers' deaths was an avalanche. In spite of this, the mystery of the Dyatlov Pass Incident continues to capture the public imagination. Books, documentaries, and fictional adaptations abound, and the mystery is still unsolved as far as many are concerned.

053. Amelia Earhart's Last Flight

What happened to Amelia Earhart?

Amelia Earhart was a legendary pilot and a pioneering aviator, known for her daring spirit and many record-breaking feats. One of her major accomplishments was in 1928, when she became the first female pilot to fly solo across the Atlantic Ocean. In 1937, she set out on her most ambitious adventure yet: she wanted to be the first woman to fly around the world. But the flight would end in tragedy.

Earhart's route began in Oakland, California and went west to east. It was unannounced, though, and it was only after she reached Miami, Florida on the 1st of June that she revealed her plans to the public.

After about a month of flying, on July 2, Earhart and her navigator, Fred Noonan, departed from Lae Airfield in Papua, New Guinea and set off for Howland Island, a tiny speck of land in the Pacific Ocean. It would have been the final leg of their journey before completing the trip around the globe, but they never arrived at Howland Island. In spite of extensive search efforts, no wreckage or signs of their plane were ever found.

Some believe that their plane ran out of fuel and crashed into the ocean, while others have suggested that Earhart and Noonan were captured by militant Japanese forces, or landed on a remote island and ultimately perished. One particularly notorious claim was that Earhart survived the flight, moved to New Jersey, and assumed a new identity, as Irene Bolam! The real Irene Bolam filed a lawsuit against the claim, and it was quickly debunked.

One of the most widely accepted theories is that Earhart and Noonan crash-landed on Nikumaroro, a remote coral atoll in the Pacific.

Artifacts found on the atoll and Earhart's last radio transmissions suggest some support for this theory, but none of it is conclusive proof.

Amelia Earhart's disappearance left an indelible mark on aviation history and popular culture. As an aviator, Earhart continues to inspire generations of adventurers around the world. The search for her goes on, as modern technology and forensic techniques offer new ways to explore the Pacific, but the mystery of Amelia Earhart's final flight remains as elusive as ever.

054. The Past Life of Dorothy Eady

Dorothy Eady's story begins in London, where she was born in 1904. At the age of three, she suffered a near-fatal fall down a flight of stairs, after which she exhibited unusual behavior, such as foreign accent syndrome, and as she grew older claimed to have memories of a past life as an ancient Egyptian priestess named Bentreshyt. She also began to show an uncanny knowledge of Egyptian history and culture without having previous knowledge of it.

In 1931, Dorothy moved to Cairo, Egypt with her husband, where she felt an immediate sense of belonging, announcing that she had come home to stay. The couple had a son but separated in 1935 when her husband accepted a teaching job in Iraq. Dorothy and her son remained in Egypt, however. Years later, she settled in the village of Abydos near the ancient temple of the pharaoh Seti I and dedicated her life to studying and preserving Egypt's cultural heritage.

Dorothy's knowledge of ancient Egypt was incredible for her time, and she made many important contributions to Egyptology through her work as a translator and researcher. She claimed to have been given help and insights from the spirit of Seti I himself, in the form of an entity called Hor-Ra.

While Dorothy's devotion to ancient Egypt earned her some respect and admiration, the academic community didn't take kindly to her claims of reincarnation and receiving messages from spirits. For her part, Dorothy didn't waver in her claims and simply continued her work. When she moved to Abydos, she became known as *Omm Sety*, meaning "Mother of Sety," as it was customary in Egyptian villages to refer to a mother by the name of her eldest child.

Could Omm Sety have truly been a vessel for the soul of the priestess Bentreshyt? Her story raises intriguing questions about the nature of consciousness, memory, and the reality of reincarnation.

055. The Disappearance of Ambrose Bierce

Ambrose Bierce was a prolific American author known for his wit, satire, and dark horror tales. Born in 1842, Bierce gained fame for his short stories, such as "An Occurrence at Owl Creek Bridge" and "The Devil's Dictionary." But in 1913, he disappeared somewhere in Mexico, leaving behind a legacy of literary brilliance coupled with unanswered questions.

Bierce was 71 years old when he vanished. He had told friends and family earlier that he intended to travel to Mexico, which was in the middle of a revolution at the time. Bierce wanted to see the conflict firsthand, possibly as inspiration for his next story, but he never returned to write it.

Although the authorities and journalists searched for him, no trace of Bierce was ever found, and so his disappearance remains one of the great mysteries in American literary history. Some believe he met with foul play or perished in the chaos of the Mexican Revolution. One such theory suggests that he was executed by a firing squad, a fate which he believed, as he wrote in his final letters, would be a preferred dramatic ending to his life. Others theorize that he staged his own disappearance to escape personal or financial troubles, with some even suggesting he committed suicide in the desert.

Regardless of how he vanished and presumably died, Ambrose Bierce's works have captivated readers over the years with their dark humor, keen insight, and unflinching glimpses into the human condition. He himself has appeared in several stories, and has inspired many great authors, from Kurt Vonnegut to Robert Heinlein.

For over a century, scholars have wondered what became of the esteemed writer. Did he meet his end in the Mexican wilderness, or did he find refuge in some obscure village? The truth may never be uncovered.

056. The Tunguska Event

On June 30, 1908, an explosion occurred near the Tunguska River in Siberia, Russia. Eyewitnesses said they saw a blinding flash of light followed by a shockwave that flattened trees and scorched the earth for miles around. The force of the blast was estimated to be more than 1,000 times the power of the atomic bomb that would be dropped on Hiroshima a few decades later!

The Tunguska Event is estimated to have knocked down 80 million trees over an area of more than 2,000 square kilometers. But although the explosion was so immensely powerful, it is believed there were at most three casualties, as the region was very remote and only sparsely populated.

So what was the cause of the Tunguska Event? The most widely accepted hypothesis is that the explosion was a meteor or comet air burst, which occurs when a small asteroid or comet explodes after entering the atmosphere of a planet. The friction from particles in the atmosphere causes the incoming ball of rock to be heated to extremely high temperatures.

While scientists and researchers widely accept the meteor air burst theory, there have also been more outlandish explanations put forward to explain the Tunguska Event. Some have suggested that the explosion was caused by a crashed alien spacecraft, a mid-air collision with a UFO, and even the implosion of a miniature black hole! Most of these theories lack credible evidence though.

Such an explosion can release an incredible amount of energy, but since the rock explodes in the atmosphere, it doesn't leave behind a crater like a meteorite strike would. This has left many scientists intrigued about the exact nature of the object that exploded above Tunguska, and how it even arrived on Earth to begin with. After all, the explosion wiped out all traces of it, at least that we know of. To this day, the area around Tunguska is still being searched for clues as to the origin of the explosion and for potential glimpses into the secrets of our universe.

057. The Babushka Lady

On November 22, 1963, as President John F. Kennedy's motorcade passed through Dealey Plaza in Dallas, Texas, there were many who witnessed the fatal shooting of the beloved president by Lee Harvey Oswald. Among them was a woman wearing a headscarf who ultimately captured the attention of both investigators and conspiracy theorists.

The Babushka Lady was named after the style of the headscarf she wore, one that was common among Russian elderly women, or "babushkas." She was seen in several photographs and in film footage taken in Dealey Plaza on the day of the assassination. She appeared to be holding a camera and filming the events as they unfolded. But even with the footage and many efforts by investigators to identify her, her identity remains shrouded in mystery to this day.

Over the years since the assassination, many women have come forward claiming to be the mysterious figure. One of them was Beverly Oliver, whose testimony was used in documentaries and films about the event. However, she claimed to have used a camera that wasn't even made until several years after the assassination, which—along with other inconsistencies—cast doubt on her claims.

So who was the Babushka Lady? While some believe she was simply a witness among the crowds that day, others think she may have been a spy for the Russians. Many conspiracy theories go further, speculating that she may have been part of a larger plot to cover up the identity of the real assassin and divert attention toward Oswald.

Whether a key witness, Russian spy, or just an innocent bystander, the true identity of the Babushka Lady remains one of the many mysteries of the Kennedy assassination even today.

058. The Mad Gasser of Mattoon

In the late summer and fall of 1944, the small town of Mattoon, Illinois, was gripped by fear as reports emerged of a mysterious assailant called the Mad Gasser, who attacked his victims with some kind of toxic gas. Descriptions of the Gasser varied, with some witnesses claiming to have seen a tall, thin man wearing dark clothes and a tight cap, while others reported a cloaked figure carrying a device that looked like a flit gun (a hand-pumped insecticide sprayer).

Victims of the Mad Gasser said they experienced a range of disturbing symptoms, including coughing fits, nausea, dizziness, and even temporary paralysis. Some even claimed to have seen a strange, sweet-smelling gas leaking out from their homes or through their open windows before falling ill. Thankfully, nobody died or had any long-term effects from the attacks.

The reports of the Mad Gasser sent the town of Mattoon into a panic, as residents barricaded themselves indoors and armed themselves against the threat of the frightening figure. Police looked into the incidents, but the elusive Gasser remained at large, leaving behind a trail of fear.

The police who investigated the incidents were themselves skeptical about whether he existed. Theories behind the attacks range from mass hysteria to the actions of a lone prankster or criminal. Some believe that the Gasser may have been a product of wartime anxiety, while others suggest that the attacks may have been the work of a mentally ill individual who wanted to cause havoc.

Despite extensive investigations by police and forensics experts, the case remains a puzzling unsolved mystery. Even today, no one can say whether the Mad Gasser was a real threat, or simply an imagined one brought on by mass hysteria during wartime.

059. The Disappearance of Judge Crater

Judge Joseph Force Crater, born in 1889, was a New York Supreme Court Justice known for his charm, wit, and connections to the underworld. On the evening of August 6, 1930, he stepped into a New York City cab on West 45th Street after having dinner at Billy Haas' Chophouse… and was never seen again!

His disappearance didn't immediately cause a stir, though. He and his wife had been vacationing at their summer cabin in Maine when he left her on August 3 to travel to New York City on business, promising to return for her birthday on August 9. But ten days later, when he still had not returned, his wife began calling their friends in New York to ask if anyone had seen him.

Judge Crater's sudden and unexplained disappearance sent shockwaves through New York City, and the legal system in particular, and even drew the attention of the rest of the nation. The initial investigation found that his personal belongings in his apartment, as well as his safe deposit box, had also gone missing, but although some leads trickled in over the months that followed, none led anywhere conclusive. He was declared dead in 1939, and the case was finally closed in 1979.

Many theories have tried to explain Judge Crater's disappearance. Some believe he was the victim of foul play, and may have been silenced by powerful figures in the criminal underworld he was known to have ties to. Others think he staged his own disappearance to escape his growing legal and financial troubles.

The case of Judge Crater's disappearance has been told in multiple books, movies, and TV shows that have reviewed the various theories surrounding the event. For a time, the phrase "to pull a Judge Crater" meant to disappear. Whether victim or mastermind of his own vanishing act, the fate of Judge Crater remains an intriguing page in American history.

060. The Sleeping Sickness

Encephalitis Lethargica, sometimes referred to as the Sleeping Sickness, first broke out in the years following World War I. Between 1916 and 1931, more than a million people around the world suddenly fell victim to a strange illness that attacked the brain, often leaving patients unable to speak or move, like living statues!

Those who were infected by the Sleeping Sickness experienced a wide range of symptoms, including high fever, sore throat, headache, double vision, slowed reactions, lethargy, and even catatonia and muscle paralysis. Some patients remained in a near-coma state for weeks or even years, while others experienced involuntary movements, tremors, and mental disturbances.

The cause of the Sleeping Sickness has confounded medical experts and researchers for decades. In spite of extensive investigations both during and after the epidemic, no single pathogen or environmental factor has been definitively linked to the outbreak. While some other infectious diseases, such as the Spanish Flu and influenza were thought to indirectly lead to the Sleeping Sickness, these connections were proved by modern research to be flimsy.

Treatment options were limited, and often not effective. While some patients improved a little after taking stimulants or receiving supportive care, many others were left permanently disabled or died later from complications caused by the illness. It is believed that at least 500,000 people died from the effects of the disease!

By the late 1920s, the number of new cases of Sleeping Sickness began to decline, and most people began to believe that the outbreak had run its course. However, isolated cases continued to occur from time to time for decades, even up until today, but the true cause of the illness is still a mystery. Though the outbreak may have faded from public memory, its legacy lives on as a cautionary tale of the unpredictable nature of infectious diseases, as we were recently reminded by the COVID-19 pandemic.

061. The Circleville Letters

In the late 1970s, residents of Circleville, Ohio began receiving mysterious and threatening anonymous letters. The letters were filled with menacing messages, threats, and accusations against the recipients. What was most terrifying was that whoever wrote them knew deeply personal details about the recipients' lives.

Although the sheriff and local law enforcement investigated the matter, the identity of the Circleville Letter Writer remained elusive. The letters continued to arrive in the hundreds, each written in an unrecognizable blocky script, leading to fear and paranoia in the tight-knit community.

The letters took a deadly turn when Mary Gillespie, a school bus driver, received a letter threatening her life over an affair she was having. Mary's husband, Ron Gillespie, set off in a truck, claiming to know who had sent her the letters, and was killed in a car crash on his way to confront the supposed writer. It was thought that his death may not have been accidental, however, because a recently fired gun was found near his body.

Some theorized that the author of the Circleville Letters was a disgruntled resident seeking revenge or attention, while others thought there might have been a cover-up or vendetta that involved multiple people. In the end, Ron's brother-in-law, Paul Freshour, was believed to be the letter writer, based on handwriting analysis and some evidence found in the home of the Gillespies. He was tried and convicted of the attempted murder of Mary and sentenced to prison. However, while he was behind bars, the letters continued to appear, with some even addressed to Freshour himself! They finally stopped when he was released from prison after serving ten years.

After decades of investigation, the true identity of the Circleville Letter Writer is still a question mark as far as many are concerned.

062. The Disappearance of DB Cooper

He hijacked a plane and got what he wanted from his victims, only to disappear into the night of the Pacific Northwest. What was the true fate of DB Cooper?

On November 24, 1971, a man going by the name of Dan Cooper got on board Northwest Orient Airlines Flight 305, set to fly from Portland, Oregon, to Seattle, Washington. Dressed in a suit and tie, Cooper calmly handed a note to a flight attendant during the flight, claiming to have a bomb in his briefcase, and demanded $200,000 in ransom and four parachutes.

After landing in Seattle to collect the ransom money and parachutes in exchange for the other passengers, Cooper ordered the plane to take off again, directing it to fly to Mexico City at a low altitude. But about half an hour after takeoff, somewhere over the rugged terrain of the Pacific Northwest, Cooper parachuted from the rear staircase of the plane into the night and disappeared without a trace.

His name became DB Cooper when one of the journalists who first reported the story confused him with another suspect, and so began the legend of DB Cooper. In the years that followed the hijacking, the FBI maintained an active case file on him and conducted extensive investigations and manhunts. But neither Cooper nor the ransom money was ever found again.

What could have happened to DB Cooper after he jumped into the night over the forests of southwestern Washington state? The FBI suspected that Cooper did not survive the jump due to the bad weather that night and the harsh, unfamiliar terrain he landed in. They also surmised that he wouldn't have been wearing suitable clothes to survive in the region for long. Others believe that he successfully escaped and lived out his days under another false identity.

The legend of DB Cooper has captivated the public imagination ever since. Numerous books, movies, and TV shows have focused on the incident and offered theories about who he was and what happened to him. His feat also inspired several copycat hijackers, which resulted in upgrades to security on commercial airlines. Though more than 50 years have passed, the true identity and fate of DB Cooper are still the subject of much debate to this day.

063. The Black Dahlia Murder

Elizabeth Short was an aspiring 22-year-old actress from Boston, Massachusetts, whose life came to a tragic end in January 1947. Her body was found mutilated in a vacant lot in Los Angeles, California one morning, sparking one of the most notorious murder investigations in American history. As was the custom at the time, due to the brutal nature of her death, the newspapers gave her a haunting nickname: the Black Dahlia.

The most shocking detail of the state in which Short's body was found was that she was naked and cut in half. The killer had also disfigured her body in other ways, and even "posed" it in a grotesque manner. The investigation into the Black Dahlia murder was extensive, with the LAPD, the FBI, and reporters working tirelessly to uncover the perpetrator. More than 150 suspects were produced in the course of the investigation, and several others even confessed to the crime! However, due to a lack of conclusive evidence, none of the suspects were ever formally charged, and the case remains unsolved to this day.

Was the Black Dahlia murder the work of a serial killer, or was it something else? Short's murder occurred during a span of years when several other young women in Los Angeles were found abused and murdered in a serial fashion. But because Short was an attractive young actress, some think it may have been a crime of passion or the result of an extortion attempt gone fatally wrong.

The Black Dahlia murder continues to puzzle investigators and amateur sleuths alike and has been explored in many books, films, and TV shows that focus on true crime. The gruesome nature of the murder, coupled with the lack of closure for everyone involved, has made it one of the most fascinating mysteries in American criminal history.

064. The Hopkinsville Goblins

On the evening of August 21, 1955, a group of residents of a farmhouse in rural Hopkinsville, Kentucky, made a very unusual claim at their local police station: they said they had encountered strange, small creatures with glowing yellow eyes and large pointed ears, and that the beings had attacked their farmhouse for hours after emerging from a nearby spaceship!

According to their account, the creatures had terrorized their farmhouse throughout the night, repeatedly trying to get inside by popping up on the doorways or peeking through the windows. Although the adults had tried to scare off the creatures by firing their guns at them, they were unable to drive them away.

Local law enforcement immediately headed to the farmhouse to investigate but found no evidence that any of the little creatures or a spaceship had ever existed, though they did find fresh bullet holes in the windows and door frames, and other traces of gunfire.

Word of the bizarre incident quickly spread and attracted the attention of the media. UFOlogists, in particular, claim it to be one of the most significant sightings of UFOs yet. Because of how much the description of the creatures resembled gremlins from folklore, they came to be known as the Hopkinsville Goblins. Some have even suggested that the creatures were goblins from a fantasy world!

Skeptics have very different theories, of course. They believe that the farmhouse residents had mistaken some of the local wildlife for aliens. One likely candidate was the great horned owls in the area, which have pointed ears and yellow eyes. Others suggest the residents had hallucinated due to stress or because they were drunk.

The story of the Hopkinsville Goblins spread throughout the world of paranormal enthusiasts and conspiracy theorists everywhere. The incident has been the subject of books, documentaries, TV shows, and films, since the truth has never been definitively proven.

065. The Somerton Man

In December 1948, the body of an unidentified man was discovered on Somerton Beach near Adelaide, South Australia. Wearing a suit and tie, with no identification on his person, the man's death and the confounding evidence on him would turn into one of Australia's most talked-about murder mysteries.

The most important clue found on the body of the Somerton Man was a piece of paper found in his pocket with the words "Tamám Shud" printed on it, which is how the incident also came to be referred to as the Tamám Shud Case. The phrase is Persian, and translates to "it is finished" or "it is over." The paper was found to have been torn from a copy of *Rubaiyat of Omar Khayyám*, a book of poetry by the 12th-century Persian polymath (one whose knowledge covers a wide span of subjects) Omar Khayyám.

When investigators found and examined the book from which the "Tamám Shud" phrase was torn, they discovered a series of encrypted letters and numbers written in the margins. Despite extensive efforts to break the code, the meaning of the cipher remains unsolved to this day. This only added to the mystery of the Somerton Man's identity.

Many theories have been proposed to explain the fate of the British-looking Somerton Man. One widely accepted belief is that he was a Cold War spy who was assassinated while on a mission, although others have suggested that he may have been involved in illegal activities. There are even those who think he was part of an elaborate hoax.

The truth behind this mysterious incident remains unknown all these years later. Even recent attempts to use DNA analysis to determine the identity of the man resulted in inconclusive leads. Whether a victim of foul play or an agent in a clandestine operation gone wrong, the Somerton Man's story is one of Australia's most famous enigmas.

066. The Disappearance of Jimmy Hoffa

Those who get on the wrong side of the Mafia often deal with terrible consequences. Was this the fate of Jimmy Hoffa as well?

Jimmy Hoffa, born in 1913, rose to prominence as a powerful leader in the American labor movement, most notably serving as president of the union known as the International Brotherhood of Teamsters from 1957 to 1971. His outsized personality, unscrupulous methods, and involvement in various controversies made him a polarizing figure in American society. Then, on July 30, 1975, he became notorious for a very different reason.

That afternoon, Hoffa was set to meet with leaders of the New York City and Detroit Mafia at the Machus Red Fox restaurant in Bloomfield Township, Michigan. After arriving, he made some calls to his wife and other friends, complaining that the Mafia had stood him up. He was last seen pacing outside the restaurant—and was never seen or heard from again.

Due to his past as a union leader, his political influence, and his dealings with the mob, his mysterious disappearance became one of the biggest missing person cases in American history. Several law enforcement agencies were involved, including the FBI, but Hoffa's body was never recovered, no solid leads were found, and Hoffa was declared legally dead in 1982.

The most common theory behind Hoffa's disappearance is that he was the victim of a Mafia hit. He had been trying to reclaim his position of power in the Teamsters Union at the time, and in doing so had angered some key members of the Mafia, including the leaders he was supposed to meet on the day he vanished! But a mix of solid alibis, conflicting claims, and missing evidence all allowed the Mafia to dodge any criminal charges, even though they may not have avoided suspicion from the general public at large.

The fate of Jimmy Hoffa has become the subject of numerous books, movies, and conspiracy theories, with new theories and speculations emerging regularly to fuel public fascination with the case, but the truth behind Hoffa's disappearance will likely never be discovered.

067. The Gardner Museum Heist

On March 18, 1990, two men who said they were police officers responding to a disturbance call were let into the Isabella Stewart Gardner Museum in Boston, Massachusetts. Once inside, they committed one of the largest art thefts in American history, making off with 13 works of art that were never recovered again.

The selection of the pieces was quite bizarre. While one of the paintings was *The Concert* by Johannes Vermeer, thought to be the most valuable unrecovered painting in the world, and some of the others were by renowned artists like Rembrandt and Edgar Degas, a few of the pieces that were stolen are relatively valueless, and more priceless paintings in the museum were left untouched. The total value of the stolen items was estimated at over $500 million. The museum staff put empty frames in their place, as they were intended to be permanent exhibits, leaving a noticeable void in the museum's collection.

Although the Boston police and the FBI launched a number of investigations into the theft, most of the questions surrounding the Gardner Museum heist remain unanswered. Who were the thieves, and what drove them to target the museum? Where are the stolen artworks now, and will they ever be recovered?

Some believe that the theft was orchestrated by members of the Boston Mafia or other gangs in the city, although they denied any involvement, and Boston's law enforcement didn't find any evidence against them. Other theories suggest that it may have been an inside job involving museum staff or security personnel.

The heist has spawned books, documentaries, and a number of theories, all of which have kept the case in the public eye and fueled speculation about the fate of the stolen artworks. The museum offers a $10 million reward for any information that could lead to the recovery of the artwork, but it has yet to be claimed!

068. The Lead Masks Case

The bodies of two Brazilian electronic technicians were discovered on August 20, 1966, on a hillside in Rio de Janeiro. One of the bizarre clues found at the site were the lead masks on their faces, which led to the name of one of the most intriguing mysteries in Brazilian history.

The two men, Manoel Pereira da Cruz and Miguel José Viana, were found lying next to one another. They each wore a formal suit, a lead mask similar to those worn as protection against radiation, and a waterproof coat. Other odd clues included an empty water bottle and a packet of wet towels.

Possibly the strangest clue of all was a small notebook containing the following cryptic instructions (translated from Portuguese): "16:30 be at the specified location. 18:30 ingest capsules, after the effect protect metals await signal mask."

There were no signs of violence on the bodies, and autopsies revealed that they had likely died from asphyxiation, but couldn't determine what had caused them to lose oxygen in the first place. Because the coroner's office was overworked at the time, the bodies were only autopsied weeks after they were found, and their internal organs were too decomposed to be reliably tested, so the exact cause of death was never found.

Multiple theories have been put forward to explain the Lead Masks case. Some believe that da Cruz and Viana were in a secret society or cult that required them to perform a ritual with the masks. They could also have died from a fatal overdose of a drug associated with the ritual. More outlandish theories suggest that they may have been victims of a failed experiment, or even contact with hostile aliens! Whatever the truth, the mystery of the Lead Masks has captured the imaginations of true crime enthusiasts and paranormal investigators around the world.

069. The Coral Castle

The Coral Castle, located in Homestead, Florida, was the life's work of one man: Edward Leedskalnin. Born in Latvia in 1887, Leedskalnin emigrated to the United States in the early 20th century and spent over 28 years single-handedly constructing the Coral Castle out of massive limestone blocks.

Using only hand tools and primitive equipment, Leedskalnin carved and sculpted over 1000 tonnes of coral rock to create the Coral Castle. The massive stones were carefully arranged without mortar to form many intricate structures, including an 8-foot tall revolving gate, an accurate sundial, a fountain, and a throne room with a table in the shape of Florida. The stones are put together with such precision that light doesn't pass through any of the joints!

What makes the Coral Castle truly remarkable is not just its scale, but the mystery of how it was even made to begin with—and by one man, no less. Leedskalnin claimed to have discovered the secrets of antigravity, reverse magnetism, and other supernatural abilities, which he presumably used to move the massive stones with ease. However, the exact methods he used are still a subject of debate and speculation. When asked about them, he would simply say, "It's not difficult if you know how."

While some believe the claims that he possessed supernatural abilities or some knowledge of ancient technologies, others suggest that he simply made use of ingenious tricks with physics principles to put it all together. For example, the impressive balance and smoothness of the revolving gate was found to be due to a metal shaft and an old truck bearing Leedskalnin had inserted inside the structure.

The Coral Castle continues to mystify visitors, attracting tourists, researchers, and amateur sleuths from around the world, as the secrets behind most of its construction remain elusive.

070. The Mystery of Elisa Lam

On January 31, 2013, a 21-year-old Canadian student named Elisa Lam vanished while staying at the Stay on Main Hotel in downtown Los Angeles. Although she was reported missing by her parents on February 8, her disappearance gained international attention on February 13, when the LAPD released surveillance footage of her in the hotel's elevator. Her creepy behavior inside the elevator made the video a viral hit.

The unsettling surveillance footage, which lasted around two and a half minutes, showed Elisa Lam making erratic movements, pressing multiple buttons, peeking out into the hallway, and gesturing as if she were talking to someone not seen in the video.

Some days later, guests at the hotel complained of low water pressure in their rooms, and a few said that their water was black with an unusual taste. On February 19, when a hotel maintenance worker checked the water tanks on the building's roof, he found Elisa Lam's body inside one of them. Her death was ruled an accident, even though her autopsy was mostly inconclusive.

It soon became known that Elisa Lam had been suffering from bipolar disorder, which was added as a contributing factor to her death. But many questions remained about her demise: Was her behavior inside the elevator due to a psychotic episode, drugs, or something else? The video's timestamp was obscured, and many claimed it had been tampered with in other ways. Could it have shown another person inside the elevator, perhaps even her killer? How did she get onto the roof, and into one of the heavily protected water tanks? And had she been alone at the time?

Elisa Lam's mysterious death continues to be the subject of documentaries, podcasts, and online forums for amateur sleuths and conspiracy theorists more than 10 years later.

071. The Pollock Twins

The Pollock family in Hexham, England, suffered an unimaginable tragedy in May 1957, when their two young daughters were tragically killed while walking to church, when they were struck by a suicidal driver on drugs. The two girls, Joanna and Jacqueline, were eleven and six at the time, and their parents, John and Florence Pollock, were devastated.

A year later, in October 1958, Florence gave birth to twin daughters Gillian and Jennifer. Oddly enough, the two little girls behaved in a strikingly similar way to their deceased sisters, and Jennifer even had birthmarks in the same places as Jacqueline .

The family moved to Whitley Bay shortly after they were born, but Gillian and Jennifer would talk about places and experiences in Hexham that they couldn't possibly have known about. They also remembered the toys that Joanna and Jacqueline had played with, and even enjoyed the same kinds of food and games.

While John believed in reincarnation, Florence was skeptical, until she heard the twins talking about the car accident one night, even though neither parent had told them about it. The case of the Pollock Twins soon grabbed the attention of researchers and experts in the field of reincarnation and the paranormal. Investigators interviewed the family and kept a record of the twins' memories and behaviors as they tried to explain their link to their deceased sisters.

While believers in the supernatural are convinced the twins were the new vessels of the reincarnated Joanna and Jacqueline, or shared some other kind of deep spiritual connection, skeptics have suggested that Gillian and Jennifer had simply been told about their siblings by their four elder brothers and, as a result, adopted similar behaviors. Whatever the truth, the case of the Pollock Twins still draws the attention of believers and skeptics alike.

072. The Oakville Blobs

In August 1994, residents of Oakville, Washington, were startled to discover gelatinous blobs that had fallen from the sky after a rainstorm. The blobs were translucent and jelly-like in appearance and varied in size from half the size of a rice grain to the size of peas. This peculiar event would become known as the Oakville Blobs incident.

Shortly after the blobs fell from the sky, some residents reported experiencing a bizarre range of symptoms, including nausea, dizziness, and early signs of the flu. Some pets died in the days that followed, and some people even claimed to have suffered from respiratory issues and temporary blindness! The blobs were blamed for all of this, and their mysterious nature left many of the townsfolk baffled and concerned.

Local authorities collected samples of the blobs for analysis, but the results only added to the mystery. The blobs were initially said to contain human white blood cells, but further tests disproved this. Still, other than two species of bacteria that were not harmful to humans, no other organic matter or identifiable substances were found.

The more sensational theories about the blobs suggest they were the result of military experiments or secret government testing, or that they could have been extraterrestrial or even divine in nature. Even some of the more mundane possibilities are quite disturbing, such as the hypothesis that they are the remains of dead jellyfish that were evaporated into a rain cloud.

The true origin of the blobs remains a mystery, as do the effects they had on the residents of Oakville. Years of investigation by researchers have not turned up anything conclusive. Whether a natural phenomena or something more puzzling, the Oakville Blobs will likely continue to befuddle investigators for years to come.

073. Flight MH370

A simple passenger flight became a source of international drama when it went wildly off its course and then vanished. What happened to flight MH370?

On March 8, 2014, Malaysia Airlines Flight MH370 took off from Kuala Lumpur International Airport on a routine flight to Beijing, China. However, less than an hour into the flight, the aircraft vanished from radar screens without a trace, sparking one of the largest and most extensive search efforts in aviation history.

In the days and weeks following the disappearance of Flight MH370, search and rescue teams from around the world scoured the vast expanse of the South China Sea, the Andaman Sea, and the southern Indian Ocean, looking for wreckage or any sign of the missing plane.

Despite all efforts, the resting place of the aircraft was never found, although some debris from the plane washed up on the shores of the western Indian Ocean in 2015 and 2016.

As the search for Flight MH370 continued, new clues and leads emerged, but these led to dead ends, conflicting information, and false hopes. Satellite data indicated that the plane may have continued flying for several hours after it disappeared from radar, but its exact whereabouts could not be tracked.

What could have happened to Flight MH370? And why did it veer so far away from its intended course? Some think that it may have been hijacked or sabotaged, while others speculate that it may have experienced mechanical failure or been brought down by pilot error. Many of the passengers were Chinese, which prompted criticism from the Chinese public at the slow rate at which information was recovered.

Despite years of investigation and analysis, the fate of Flight MH370 and the 239 people on board remains one of the greatest modern mysteries in aviation history. The lack of physical evidence and the mostly inconclusive clues that were found left investigators and families of the victims frustrated and bewildered. The disappearance of Flight MH370 serves as a sobering reminder of the fragility of life and the fact that even in this age of modern technology, catastrophic and mystifying events can happen anywhere.

CHAPTER 4: SCIENTIFIC MYSTERIES

074. Dark Matter and Dark Energy

Dark matter is a perplexing substance that makes up about 27% of the universe's mass. It neither gives out nor reflects light—which is how it gets its name—but this also makes it invisible to telescopes. We know that it exists because of the gravitational force it exerts on the things we *can* see, like stars and galaxies.

What could dark matter consist of? Scientists think it may be exotic types of particles that interact weakly with the matter we're more familiar with, such as protons and electrons. Researchers have recreated some of these interactions in the lab with special detectors, and have tried to create and study dark matter itself using particle colliders. But even with these efforts, and a continuing search for other methods of study, its true nature remains elusive.

Dark energy may have a similar name, but it is very much its own phenomenon, and makes up around 68% of the universe's energy. Unlike dark matter, which pulls objects toward it, dark energy pushes outward, and it's causing the universe to expand at an accelerated rate. Scientists discovered this after observing distant supernovae (exploding stars), whose constant amount of light emitted make for good markers when measuring cosmic distances.

Like dark matter, dark energy cannot be observed directly using our current technology, and scientists can only speculate about what it could be. Some think dark energy is an energy linked to the vacuum of space itself, also called the cosmological constant. Others believe it is a net result of various energy fields that are scattered throughout space, also referred to as scalar fields. Scientists hope to learn more about dark energy by observing how distant galaxies move with time, as well as fluctuations in CMB radiation (the leftover energy from the Big Bang event that gave rise to the universe).

What is the true nature of dark matter and dark energy, and how do they shape the cosmos? The answers are as yet unknown, but the quest to unlock their secrets will continue for years to come.

075. The Wow! Signal

On August 15, 1977, astronomer Jerry R. Ehman detected an unusual signal while working on the SETI project at Ohio State University's Big Ear radio telescope. SETI stands for Search for Extra-Terrestrial Intelligence, and its purpose is exactly that. The signal, which lasted for 72 seconds, was unusually strong and appeared to come from the direction of the constellation Sagittarius. Ehman was so astonished by the signal that he circled it on the printout and wrote "Wow!" next to it, which is how it got its iconic name.

Strong though it was, the Wow! signal has never been detected again. Over the years, scientists have used everything from more sensitive radio telescopes to observatories built in space to scan the cosmos, searching for similar signals or other strange events like it that could offer additional clues to its origin. But without a repeat performance, finding the source and the true nature of the Wow! signal has become one of the most significant challenges in modern astronomy. Adding to the mystery is the fact that no other detectors on Earth received the signal, even more sensitive ones.

Given that it was discovered through the SETI project, it has inevitably been thought of as a communication from aliens, although those who believe this are as yet unsure of what the message, assuming it was one, could have been.

Other theories suggest it could have been caused by a variety of other phenomena, from a burst in naturally-occurring cosmic noise, to emissions from a passing comet or some other unidentified object in space, to even interference caused by our own technology on Earth. However, none of the explanations have managed to account for all the peculiarities in the Wow! signal.

Regardless of its origin, the Wow! signal continues to fascinate astronomers and cosmos enthusiasts everywhere, who hope that someday we will uncover the truth behind this cosmic mystery.

076. The Fermi Paradox

Based on the odds, the chances of alien life in our galaxy are extremely high. So why does it feel like we might be the only intelligent life in the universe?

Enrico Fermi was a physicist who helped create the world's first nuclear reactor and was called "the architect of the nuclear age" for his work. In the summer of 1950, when discussing UFO reports with fellow physicists, he famously asked the question: "But where is everybody?" This is the Fermi Paradox in its simplest form.

Given the sheer number of stars in the universe (well over a billion!) and that each has a fair chance of having Earth-like planets that can support life, there should be plenty of intelligent alien civilizations among the stars. But after decades of searching, we still haven't found any conclusive evidence of extraterrestrial life. All we have are multiple possible solutions to the Fermi Paradox.

One suggested explanation is called the "Great Silence." According to this concept, even if life is common in the universe, the odds of it developing into highly advanced civilizations that can send and receive interstellar messages may be very low. Factors such as natural disasters, extinction events, societies collapsing, or technological limits could prevent these lifeforms from achieving the means to make their presence known.

Another possibility answer to the Fermi Paradox is that advanced civilizations may exist but are beyond our own current technological limits to detect. For example, extraterrestrial beings might be making use of methods or energies to communicate that are beyond the range of our current instruments... or even beyond our understanding of scientific principles.

The Zoo hypothesis states that alien civilizations are aware that we exist, but choose not to make contact with us, much like how visitors in a zoo do not interact with the animals on display. According to this hypothesis, these advanced aliens may be studying us from afar, waiting for us to advance to a certain level of technology before they make themselves known to us.

One of the more dramatic possibilities is the dark forest hypothesis, which suggests that after an alien civilization becomes advanced enough, it seeks to destroy other civilizations that might be a threat to its own existence. As a result, they are hesitant to reveal themselves for fear of being destroyed themselves.

While we may not have definitive answers to the Fermi Paradox yet, the quest to unravel this mystery continues to drive scientific exploration and discovery. Who knows what revelations the future may hold, and which, if any, of the varied proposed explanations will turn out to be the right one?

077. The Flyby Anomaly

When spacecraft pass close to a planet to make use of its gravitational pull or simply to observe the planet (this maneuver is also known as a flyby) they sometimes gain a slight acceleration or deceleration that cannot be accounted for by the gravity of the planet alone. This strange deviation is known as the Flyby Anomaly and has puzzled scientists since its discovery in the early '90s.

The Flyby Anomaly first caught the attention of scientists during the flybys of several spacecraft near Earth, including NASA's Galileo and NEAR spacecrafts, and the ESA's (European Space Agency) Rosetta space probe. In each case, the observed velocity of the spacecraft was different from what it should have been based on models of the planets and their gravity fields. The difference, though small, was consistent across multiple flyby missions over the years, but strangely not all similar missions.

What could be causing the Flyby Anomaly? Several explanations have been put forward, ranging from unknown gravitational effects to errors in measurements. Some scientists speculate that it could be caused by variations in how mass is distributed within the planets, which would affect how their gravitational pull is also distributed as a result. Other possibilities include the presence of dark matter interfering with the spacecraft, a side effect of space around the planet being warped by gravity, shifts in light emissions from the spacecraft that are unaccounted for, or even a kind of new physics principle beyond our current knowledge.

Scientists have conducted extensive simulations and other experiments to try to replicate the anomaly in more controlled spaces, where careful observations are easier to make, but so far, no definitive explanation has been found. And so the Flyby Anomaly remains an intriguing puzzle waiting to be solved.

With advances in technology and new missions planned to explore the outer reaches of our solar system and beyond, perhaps we will one day unravel the secrets behind this particular cosmic mystery.

078. The Kuiper Cliff

The Kuiper Belt is a vast region of icy bodies and dwarf planets located beyond Neptune's orbit. It was discovered in the early 1990s and is home to a very diverse array of celestial objects, such as the dwarf planets Pluto and Eris, and many frozen asteroids. However, astronomers noticed something peculiar about how these objects are distributed in the outer Kuiper Belt: Beyond a certain distance from the Sun, the number of objects in the belt has a mysteriously sharp drop-off.

Called the Kuiper Cliff, this steep drop in the density of the belt happens after a distance of about 50 astronomical units (AU) from the Sun (for reference, one AU is the average distance of the Earth from the Sun). This unexpected drop-off is a stark contrast from the more gradual changes in the number of objects found in the inner Kuiper Belt.

Scientists have put forward several theories to try to explain the Kuiper Cliff phenomenon. One possibility is that there is an undiscovered planet or some other massive object beyond the Kuiper Belt that could be scattering or clearing out icy bodies as it moves along its path, creating the cliff. Another theory suggests that the gravitational pull of passing stars or even galaxies may have disrupted the outer Kuiper Belt over time.

To better understand the Kuiper Cliff, astronomers have been conducting detailed examinations of the outer Kuiper Belt using both telescopes on the ground as well as observatories in space. They hope to identify and characterize the objects found past the Kuiper Cliff's edge, which might shed some light on the region's structure and what it is composed of. Whether it arises from various gravitational effects or the presence of an enigmatic cosmic phenomenon, the Kuiper Cliff proves that there are countless unsolved mysteries in our solar system's outer reaches.

079. The Solar Corona Mystery

As we know, the Sun is the main source of energy for Earth, but why is it hotter than it should be?

The solar corona is the outermost layer of the Sun's atmosphere and extends millions of kilometers into space from its surface, which is also called the photosphere. Unlike the photosphere, which emits light in the visible range, the corona emits light that is mainly in the form of ultraviolet and X-rays. Its faint, wispy appearance can be seen by the naked eye only during total solar eclipses, when the Moon appears to block out the Sun's bright disk.

One of the most puzzling aspects of the solar corona is its temperature. While the Sun's surface is about 9,900 degrees Fahrenheit, the corona's temperature soars to more than a million degrees! This stark difference in temperature defies physics as we know it, and has puzzled scientists for decades.

A few theories have tried to explain the extraordinary heat of the solar corona. One leading hypothesis suggests that magnetic fields are the key factor in the heating of the corona, through a process known as magnetic reconnection. Since the Sun is mostly made up of matter in the form of plasma, the magnetic field in its corona can become tangled and rearrange itself constantly, like pollen on the surface of a pond. When the field lines reconnect to each other, they would release energy in the form of heat into the corona.

Proving this, or any other theory, is difficult, however. Studying the solar corona presents unique problems due to its extreme temperatures and how faint it normally is. Astronomers must use special instruments like coronagraphs and spectrographs to observe the corona during total solar eclipses and from observatories in space.

The solar corona is not only a mesmerizing sight, but also the source of the solar wind (a stream of charged particles flowing out from the Sun) and solar flares (explosive bursts of light radiated by the Sun). The more we understand about the structure and behavior of the corona, the more we can predict and protect ourselves from the nastier side-effects of both of these phenomena.

080. The Missing Baryon Problem

Baryons are fundamental particles that make up much of what we see in space, from stars and planets to galaxies. However, when astronomers compare the number of baryons observed in space with the tally that is expected to exist based on our models of the early universe, they find that more than half of these particles are unaccounted for—a cosmic conundrum known as the Missing Baryon Problem.

To solve the Missing Baryon Problem, scientists have tried to find these elusive missing particles. One promising investigation involves studying the distribution of baryons in the vast cosmic web of *filaments* and *voids* in the universe. Filaments are large structures formed by groups (or *clusters*) of galaxies that "connect" to each other from our perspective, and voids are the spaces between the filaments.

Recent observations with telescopes such as the Chandra X-ray Observatory and the Atacama Large Millimeter Array (ALMA) have helped astronomers detect vast reservoirs of hot gas in the filaments, as well as cold gas clouds in galactic halos (the sphere of space around the circular disk that is most galaxies). Both of these are previously unknown sources of baryons.

One possible explanation for the Missing Baryon Problem is the process of *cosmic recycling*. As galaxies evolve over cosmic time, they emit gas through supernova explosions and galactic winds, sending streams of baryons into the space between galaxies. Eventually, this expelled gas cools and condenses to form new stars and galaxies, and the baryons are effectively recycled. The missing baryons could be in the transition between the two stages.

While astronomers have made progress in finding hidden reservoirs of baryons, the Missing Baryon Problem is far from solved. For example, we still don't know the exact mechanisms that send baryons out of galaxies and into intergalactic space. Ongoing observations and theoretical advancements will hopefully shed more light on this cosmic mystery.

081. The Theory of Everything

Since ancient times, humans have tried to understand the underlying rules of nature that cause things to behave the way they do in our reality, and in the universe as a whole. In modern physics, this has meant trying to unite the four fundamental forces: gravity, electromagnetism, the weak nuclear force, and the strong nuclear force. The Theory of Everything (or the Grand Unified Theory) is the ultimate dream: a single, cohesive, elegant framework that ties all these forces and their related physics together, which would explain… well, everything!

The search for the Theory of Everything in its current form has its roots in the pioneering work of one of the greatest minds of our time: Albert Einstein. In his later years, Einstein tried to find a unified theory that would align his theory of general relativity (which describes how gravity behaves on large scales like that of the cosmos) with the principles of quantum mechanics (which govern how particles behave on the tiniest of scales, beyond even the atomic level). Despite his efforts, Einstein's dream was unfulfilled when he died, and has remained an unsolved mystery even after equally remarkable minds like those of Stephen Hawking and Steven Weinberg tried to crack it.

Together with quantum physics, the Standard Model of particle physics is the best model for our current understanding of three out of the four fundamental forces, but gravity is the odd force out. While the Standard Model has been successful in predicting the behavior of particles at the subatomic level, it is incomplete without a theory that can fully explain gravity within the same framework.

One promising candidate for the Theory of Everything is *string theory*. This suggests that reality at the most fundamental level is not made up of point-like particles (which the Standard Model states), but is instead made of tiny vibrating strings that partially exist in dimensions beyond the four of our reality. String theory tries to unify gravity with the other fundamental forces by describing them all as different patterns of vibration (or *vibrational modes*) of these tiny strings. However, string theory is still a work in progress, with plenty of unanswered questions and challenges it has yet to overcome.

As scientists continue to explore the frontiers of theoretical physics, the quest for the Theory of Everything persists. New ideas, such as loop quantum gravity, supersymmetry, and extra-dimensional membranes, all offer different approaches to uniting the four forces, and hold the promise of revealing deeper truths about the nature of reality in the process. While the journey may be long and arduous, the pursuit of the Theory of Everything continues to be one of the most profound and awe-inspiring endeavors in human history.

082. The Origin of Fast Radio Bursts

Fast radio bursts (FRBs) are intense bursts of radio waves from distant galaxies that flash across the sky in the blink of an eye, emitting as much energy in a few milliseconds as the Sun does in a span of days! First detected in 2007, these enigmatic signals have since become one of the most intriguing mysteries in astronomy.

After more than a decade of research, the origins of fast radio bursts are still shrouded in mystery. Various theories have been suggested to explain their source, ranging from the cataclysmic explosions of supernovae or the merging of neutron stars, to more exotic events like evaporating black holes, or even signals from advanced alien civilizations! But even the most realistic possibilities lack evidence so far.

To uncover the sources of fast radio bursts, astronomers have conducted extensive observations, using radio telescopes from all around the world. These efforts have allowed them to identify several sources, and even some repeating sources, which implies that at least some of these mysterious signals come from very energetic and constantly shifting environments in their distant galaxies.

While the repeated fast radio bursts have provided us with the most valuable clues yet, they have also raised new questions about the mechanisms that drive these cosmic phenomena. What causes the sudden bursts of radio waves? Why do some sources repeat while others do not? Could multiple different sources produce the same kind of phenomena? Scientists continue to grapple with these questions as they push the boundaries of our understanding of the universe.

With the advance of technology leading to improvements in our techniques for observing the cosmos, astronomers are on the verge of making great strides in unraveling the mystery of fast radio bursts. Future missions, such as the Canadian Hydrogen Intensity Mapping Experiment (CHIME) and the Square Kilometer Array (SKA), promise to break new ground in our understanding of these elusive cosmic signals, and may ultimately reveal their true sources.

083. Early Supermassive Black Holes

A black hole is the last stage in the life of particularly massive stars. They contract to form a region of space so dense that it warps gravity and can even prevent light from escaping. The largest kinds of black holes are called supermassive black holes, which are colossal structures usually found at the center of galaxies that can be up to a billion times the mass of our Sun.

One of the greatest puzzles surrounding supermassive black holes is the question of their origins. The evolution of stars is a process that takes several millions of years from start to finish, and black holes would generally form at the end of that long process, but astronomers have observed supermassive black holes dating back to just a few hundred million years after the Big Bang. This implies that they would have formed when most of the universe was simply clouds of particles and galaxies were only just taking shape, so how could these cosmic titans have formed so quickly?

Could they have formed through the collapse of massive stars in the early universe, which somehow went through an accelerated version of the typical life cycle of a star? Or did they emerge through the rapid collapse of gigantic gas clouds that often gave rise to early galaxies?

One suggestion for their rapid growth is a process known as *accretion*, where newly-formed black holes are able to quickly devour surrounding gas and dust. This cosmic feast would also result in the release of vast amounts of energy, along with the formation of galaxies around them.

Whatever their true origin, these early supermassive black holes have caused scientists to take a new look at our understanding of black hole formation and the timeline of the cosmos. With the help of powerful telescopes and computer simulations, astronomers today are peering deeper into the past, hoping to piece together the history of our universe.

084. Ball Lightning

Unlike the branching lines of lightning as it strikes in the sky during a typical storm, ball lightning takes the form of glowing spheres of light, ranging from a few centimeters to several meters wide, floating and whizzing through the air. Witnesses have described them as colorful, ranging from white and yellow to orange and red, and they often give out crackling or buzzing sounds. They are fleeting in nature, lasting for just over a minute at most, but they certainly leave a lasting impression!

In spite of numerous eyewitness accounts, the origins of ball lightning are still a mystery. Scientists have come up with various theories to explain how it forms in nature, including the vaporizing of silicon from the soil, electrically charged bubbles of gas, or even miniature bolts of lightning trapped inside a magnetic field. But none of these theories fully account for all the characteristics of ball lightning.

While rare in nature, ball lightning has been successfully replicated in laboratory settings. Under controlled conditions, researchers have been able to create something that closely resembles ball lightning by using bursts of high-voltage, microwave radiation, and even exploding wires. These experiments have offered valuable insight into the possible mechanisms behind ball lightning, and confirmed parts of existing theories.

As scientists continue to explore ball lightning, new theories have emerged. Some researchers suggest that it may be a complex interaction of weather conditions, electromagnetic fields, and ionized gases. Others think it could be a type of plasma formation, or even a result of exotic physics beyond our current understanding.

Capturing ball lightning in nature remains as formidable a challenge as it has always been. It is unpredictable and fleeting, which makes it difficult to study directly or for long periods of time. Technology like high-speed cameras and electromagnetic sensors offer new ways to observe and analyze ball lightning in the wild, though, and may be the key to finally unlocking its secrets.

085. The Lithium Problem

Lithium, a light and relatively rare element in the universe, is important in astrophysics, as it can be used to trace the evolution of stars and the formation of new elements from the universe's building blocks of hydrogen and helium. However, astronomers have discovered that certain old stars, known as Population II stars, show much lower levels of lithium in their atmospheres than they should. This is referred to as The Lithium Problem.

The mystery goes deeper, though. Astronomers have also found that younger stars, such as those in the Milky Way's disk, contain higher levels of lithium than their older counterparts. This difference would suggest that the lithium in stars is somehow depleted over time as stars evolve, but how, and why? Where does it go?

To unravel The Lithium Problem, scientists have turned their attention to the processes occurring within stars. Nuclear reactions deep within the cores of stars like nuclear fusion and nuclear burning can consume lithium in the process. However, current models of these processes don't fully account for the observed lack of lithium in Population II stars, which has led to ongoing speculation.

As scientists grapple with The Lithium Problem, new theories have emerged. Some propose that lithium depletion is a side effect of heat convection currents in the inner layers of stars, while others suggest that the mass lost during a star's evolution could play a role.

Stellar archaeology, the study of the early history of the universe, could offer some insights into The Lithium Problem by taking a closer look at the chemical composition of ancient stars in our galaxy. This could help astronomers reveal more about the conditions in the early universe and the processes that shape stellar evolution, and in doing so, find a lead that could explain the fate of the missing lithium in the stars.

086. The Origins of UHECRs

Ultra-high-energy cosmic rays, or UHECRs, are subatomic particles—like protons, neutrinos, and atomic nuclei—that zoom through space at incredible speeds, sometimes reaching energies millions of times greater than anything a particle accelerator on Earth can manage. These cosmic speed demons defy physics as we know it, and their sources are a tantalizing riddle for astronomers to solve.

Where do UHECRs come from? Astronomers believe they are produced by the most extreme events in the universe, such as supernovae (the explosive deaths of massive stars), the sucking in of matter by supermassive black holes at the centers (or nuclei) of galaxies, or the collisions of galaxies with one another. However, pinpointing the exact sources of UHECRs has proven to be very difficult.

Detecting and studying UHECRs is challenging because of how rare and extremely energetic they are. Special observatories, like the Pierre Auger Observatory in Argentina and the Telescope Array in Utah, use vast arrays of detectors spread over large areas to try to capture these rare cosmic rays as they slam into Earth's atmosphere. By analyzing the arrival angle and energies of these particles, scientists hope to trace them backwards (much like how police detectives can find out where a fired bullet might have come from) and piece together the puzzle of their origin.

But after decades of research, the true nature of UHECRs remains a great cosmic puzzle. While some observations have hinted at some candidates for sources, such as nearby galaxies or particularly active galactic nuclei, no definitive proof has been found as of yet.

What scientists find as they search for the origin of UHECRs may hold profound insights for our understanding of cosmic evolution, particle physics, and the nature of space and time. Whether these energetic particles come from known astrophysical events or some exotic cosmic phenomena beyond our comprehension, the quest to unlock their secrets is among the most thrilling undertakings in modern astrophysics.

087. The Birth of Plate Tectonics

The land we walk on has been shaped by large-scale forces from before the time of the dinosaurs. But when did plate tectonics first begin?

The concept of continental drift revolutionized the field of geology in the early 20th century, and gave rise to the theory of plate tectonics. According to this theory, Earth's outer layer (or crust) is divided into several rigid plates that move and interact with each other, which is what causes earthquakes, volcanoes, and the creation of continents, as well as mountain ranges like the Himalayas.

Although it has shaped Earth as we know it, the origins of plate tectonics are shrouded in mystery. Evidence from geology suggests that the process may have begun as early as 3.5 billion years ago, about a billion years after Earth itself formed. Rocks dating back to this time period show signs of being deformed and morphed by outside forces, which are signs of tectonic activity.

But what caused plate tectonics to begin in the first place? Some theories suggest that the cooling and solidifying of Earth's mantle (the layer below the crust), together with the buildup of heat and pressure due to the decay of radioactive rocks, created the conditions needed for plate tectonics to begin. Others think that the presence of water played a key role, smoothing the movement of tectonic plates against each other and allowing for processes like subduction, in which one plate sinks beneath another.

Studying other planets and moons in our solar system has also provided valuable insights into the mechanisms driving plate tectonics on Earth. Evidence of tectonic activity on Mars and icy moons like Europa and Enceladus has shown that internal heat, the composition of the crust, and the presence of water could have all influenced the onset and evolution of tectonics.

By analyzing ancient rocks with new technologies, conducting computer simulations, and studying the geology of other planets, researchers hope to determine when and why plate tectonics began, and in doing so shed more light on the colossal forces that have shaped our planet over billions of years.

088. The Cambrian Explosion

The Cambrian Explosion refers to a time during the Cambrian Period, approximately 541 to 485 million years ago, when a very unusual kind of explosion took place. Over the span of just a few million years, Earth's oceans developed an astonishing array of complex organisms, from primitive sea sponges to the first arthropods (the ancestors of insects, spiders, snails, and crustaceans, among others) and chordates (the predecessors to vertebrate animals like mammals, birds, fish, amphibians and reptiles).

Before the Cambrian Explosion, life on Earth was mostly simple, single-celled organisms like bacteria and algae. The sudden appearance of diverse and complex creatures during this period was a dramatic leap in evolutionary innovation, and effectively gave rise to all the major animal groups of today.

What could have caused such a massive boost in the diversity of the living creatures on Earth? This is regularly debated among scientists. Rising oxygen levels in the atmosphere, changes in the chemistry of oceans, and the formation of more complex ecosystems may have all provided the needed conditions for this rapid burst to happen, together with key genetic mutations and other mechanisms of evolution.

Fossils from that period have offered valuable clues about the organisms that thrived during the Cambrian Explosion. Exquisite finds from sites such as the Burgess Shale in Canada and the Chengjiang biota in China have even preserved the delicate soft tissues of ancient marine creatures. But even with these insights into the anatomy and behavior of these creatures, there is understandably a lot we still do not know about the Earth that existed hundreds of millions of years ago.

Whatever its mysterious trigger may have been, whether changes in the environment or genetic mutations, the Cambrian Explosion was *the* major event in Earth's history that laid the foundation for the rich tapestry of life that exists on Earth today.

089. The Origins of the Moon

The Moon has been a source of intrigue since ancient times, but where did it come from?

The leading explanation for the Moon's origins is the Giant Impact Hypothesis: this suggests that the Moon was formed from the debris of a massive collision that took place between Earth and a Mars-sized protoplanet named Theia during the chaotic early history of the solar system. This catastrophic event, known as the "Big Splash," is thought to have occurred around 4.5 billion years ago, at a time when the Earth itself was effectively a protoplanet that had just been formed.

According to the Giant Impact Hypothesis, the collision between Earth and Theia gave out a tremendous amount of heat and debris, which cooled and condensed to form a disk around our planet. Over time, the material in this disk pulled itself together through gravitational forces to form the Moon, which then settled into its orbit around Earth.

Evidence in favor of the Giant Impact Hypothesis includes the composition of isotopes of elements like oxygen and titanium found on the Moon, which closely match how they are found on Earth. Computer simulations of the collision that would have taken place between Earth and Theia have offered additional support for this theory. However, the manner in which this collision took place, and how the Moon formed in the aftermath, are still a subject of debate, because there are peculiarities in the composition of the Moon as compared to the Earth, as well as the way in which they spin, that are not completely accounted for. And some questions remain: Where did Theia come from? How much of the Moon is made up of Theia, and how much of it is Earth? And what kind of collision could result in the composition that the Moon has now?

Ongoing research into how the Moon was formed continues. Future lunar missions, such as NASA's Artemis program and international efforts to collect samples from the Moon's South Pole, hold the potential to unlock the secrets of our planet's celestial partner.

090. Periodic Mass Extinctions

A mass extinction is the name given to a sudden and devastating drop in the number of species of living things on Earth. Clues found in fossils have shown compelling evidence of at least five such mass extinctions throughout Earth's history. Each time, several species simply vanished from the face of the planet. Among the most famous is the Cretaceous-Paleogene (K-Pg) mass extinction around 66 million years ago, which wiped out the dinosaurs and many other forms of life.

One of the most curious features of these mass extinctions is that they are unusually regular. According to some researchers, each event has happened between 26 to 30 million years after the previous one. This intriguingly pattern has led scientists to look at the cosmos for potential causes, such as meteoric impacts, supernovae, or regular passages through volatile parts of galactic space. To date, there has been no explanation that covers every known mass extinction.

A leading hypothesis for the cause of these extinction events is impacts from outer space. The dinosaurs were famously killed off by the Chicxulub asteroid impact in the Yucatán Peninsula in Mexico. This event has supported the idea that more catastrophic collisions with celestial bodies, like asteroids or comets, may have set off the other mass extinctions in Earth's history as well.

Another possible explanation has to do with cycles at a galactic level, such as the movement of the solar system through the Milky Way galaxy, or periodic spikes in cosmic radiation. These could potentially influence Earth's atmosphere and environment, leading to global changes in climate that result in mass extinctions. Some theories suggest that instead of the asteroid impact, it was instead a sudden change in climate that killed the dinosaurs.

While past mass extinctions have left their scars in Earth's history, scientists warn that we may be on the brink of a more unusual extinction event, this one driven by human activities like habitat destruction, pollution, and global warming. Though Earth may have endured several mass extinctions, the life on its surface has been far more fragile, which is probably a lesson worth remembering!

CHAPTER 5: CRYPTIDS, PARANORMAL, AND OTHER MYSTERIES

091. Bigfoot

Legends of Bigfoot (also known as the Sasquatch) have been passed down through generations of indigenous peoples across North America, each with their own names and descriptions of the elusive creature. Usually described as a large, hairy, ape-like being, Bigfoot is said to inhabit the remotest areas of the Canadian and American wilds.

While Bigfoot is of American origin, there have been many other similar ape-like cryptids (creatures that haven't been conclusively proven to exist yet) that appear in folktales and legends across the world. Some of these include the Skunk Ape in the swamps of Florida, the Almas in Central Asia, the Yeren in the mountains of China, the Yowie from the Australian Outback, and, as famous as Bigfoot, the Yeti in the Himalayas.

Reports of Bigfoot sightings have been documented for centuries, with people claiming to have come across the creature in forests, mountains, and even some neighborhoods in the suburbs! While many sightings were found to have been hoaxes or people mistaking other animals as Bigfoot, some have remained unresolved enough to keep the debate alive about the possible existence of an undiscovered species of ape.

After decades of expeditions and more thorough investigations, concrete evidence that Bigfoot exists has yet to be found. Researchers have collected hair samples, footprints, and photographs and videos of what appears to be the creature, but none of these have turned out to be definitive proof. Skeptics, like many of those in the scientific community, argue that without a body or solid DNA evidence, Bigfoot should be treated as a creation of myth and folklore.

That said, some scientists are still open to the possibility that new species could still be found in remote wilderness areas. But they emphasize that these findings must be proven with rigorous scientific methods and inquiry. Extraordinary claims without much proof should be treated with a healthy dose of suspicion.

Despite the lack of scientific evidence, Bigfoot continues to capture the public imagination and has inspired a thriving subculture of enthusiasts, researchers, and amateur investigators. Books, movies, TV shows, and documentaries have cemented the legend of Bigfoot and its place in popular culture for the forseeable future.

092. Out-of-Body Experiences

As the name implies, out-of-body experiences (OBEs) are when people have a sudden and profound shift in their consciousness, and see themselves as separate from their physical bodies, sometimes even seeing their surroundings from a vantage point that's outside of themselves. These can happen spontaneously or can be the result of meditation, trauma, or near-death experiences, among other things.

Psychologists and neuroscientists have come up with various explanations for OBEs, which include a sudden loss of information from the senses, states of consciousness that have been artificially altered, and medical conditions like brain injuries, seizures, or disruptions in the body's balance. Some researchers claim that OBEs may be a form of dissociation, in which the mind briefly detaches itself from the physical sensations of the body.

OBEs have a deep spiritual meaning in many cultures around the world. Practices such as astral projection, shamanic journeying, and lucid dreaming all involve altered states of mind, and the belief that the spirit can exist outside the physical body, and even transcend the bounds of time and space.

Scientists have tried to figure out the mechanisms behind OBEs, and the role played by the individual's nervous system. Neuroscience technology offers ways to analyze how the brain functions and behaves during OBEs, which can shed light on the various factors involved, such as the perception of the senses and the cognition of the brain.

Despite decades of research, OBEs have not yet been fully explained. Science has offered insights into the medical factors that play a role in OBEs, but they haven't explained the deeply personal and vivid nature of these experiences. Are they glimpses of an alternate reality? Outbursts of the subconscious mind? Echoes of an entirely new, spiritual kind of reality? Whatever the answer, out-of-body experiences continue to test our ideas of consciousness and the nature of reality.

093. The Shroud of Turin

The Shroud of Turin is a linen cloth measuring approximately 14 feet long and 3.5 feet wide that bears the faint image of the front and back of a man. It is believed by many to be the burial shroud of Jesus Christ, as the imprint on the cloth resembles Jesus' face and body, and the cloth also shows signs of wounds that are consistent with his crucifixion.

The image on the shroud is one of its most intriguing aspects. It appears to be like the negative of a film photograph, with the light and dark areas reversed. Scientists have tried to figure out how the image was created, but no explanation has yet been found. Religious folk believe that the image was created by a miracle at the moment of Jesus' resurrection, but more skeptical scholars think it may be the work of an artist using an early, undeveloped form of photography.

The exact source of the Shroud of Turin is also a subject of debate. As the burial cloth of Jesus, it would logically originate from the same time, in the 1st century CE. But others argue that it could be a medieval forgery created in the 14th century. The shroud's first recorded appearance was in the 14th century in France, and its journey before then is unknown.

The truth of the Shroud of Turin has been a source of controversy for centuries. Even the Catholic Church has neither accepted nor rejected that the shroud is the one used to bury Jesus Christ. Carbon dating tests conducted in 1988 put the shroud's age as somewhere in the medieval period, which cast doubt on its connection to Jesus. But research since then has challenged the reliability of these findings, and the debate among scholars and researchers has continued.

Whether genuine or not, the shroud continues to mystify all those familiar with it. It is a symbol of humanity's fascination with relics and artifacts that have a connection to Jesus Christ and other iconic religious figures.

094. J'Ba Fofi

Even a small spider can terrify some when it crosses their path. Could one as big as a person actually exist?

The J'Ba Fofi, which translates to "Giant Spider," is said to inhabit the dense jungles of Central Africa, particularly in the Congo Basin. Local legends from tribes like the Baka people describe it as a colossal and fearsome arachnid, with a leg span reaching up to five or six feet, maybe more! It is said to have the brown color of the jungle floor, large fangs with potent venom, and it spins massive circular webs between the trees.

Despite all the folklore and tales of J'Ba Fofi, solid evidence that it exists remains elusive beyond a few eyewitness accounts. Other than stories from local villagers, one of the more famous sightings of the spider was in 1938. Englishman Reginald Lloyd and his wife were driving through the Congolese jungle when what looked like a small monkey crossed their path. When Lloyd stopped the jeep to look through the windshield, he saw that the monkey was actually an enormous spider matching local descriptions of the J'Ba Fofi. Terrified, he floored the gas and drove away, vowing never to return to the jungle again!

Scientific expeditions into the remote reaches of the Congo Basin have found some clues about the J'Ba Fofi, such as remnants of their webs, but nothing concrete. Biologically speaking, their size appears to be impossible, since spiders have a unique system for breathing through their skin that can only function on a creature that is not much bigger than a dinner plate. As a result, some believe the legend may have developed after exaggerated or unclear sightings of known species, such as monkeys.

Others remain open to the possibility that large spiders may yet live in the unexplored depths of the Congo. With the aid of new technology, such as camera traps and aerial surveys that can open up previously inaccessible parts of the jungle, the truth behind the J'Ba Fofi may be discovered someday soon.

095. The Overtoun Bridge

Located near the village of Milton, Scotland, the Overtoun Bridge spans the Overtoun Burn gorge around 50 feet below it and offers scenic views of the countryside around it. But beneath its peaceful facade lies a strange and disturbing secret, one that has given the bridge its sinister nickname: "The Dog Suicide Bridge."

Since the 1950s, there have been several reports of dogs that have leaped from the parapet of the bridge to their deaths on the rocks below. This odd behavior gained attention again during the late 2000s and 2010s after a series of similar occurrences led to severe injuries and some deaths, puzzling experts and sparking many rumors about paranormal forces at play. Although there have been efforts to prevent further tragedies, dogs still continue to plunge from the bridge to their doom to this day!

What could explain the bizarre behavior of the dogs at Overtoun Bridge? Some believe the bridge is haunted by restless spirits. In October 1994, an infant boy was tragically killed there by a mentally ill man, which gave more support to theories about the supernatural elements at the bridge. Others think the incidents are caused by the presence of pheromones or animal scents that attract dogs to the edge of the bridge. However, no definitive explanation has been found yet.

In an effort to unravel the mystery of the Overtoun Bridge, scientists and animal behaviorists have conducted studies and experiments to understand why dogs are drawn to leap from the structure. Factors such as the height and curvature of the bridge and the presence of minks and their scents in the area have all been examined, but with no conclusive results.

The Overtoun Bridge remains a popular tourist destination in spite of the tragedies, drawing visitors from around the world who are intrigued by its eerie reputation. Local authorities have taken steps to improve safety measures and raise awareness of the dangers posed to dogs there, but the mystery of Overtoun continues to haunt the collective imagination, and the bridge itself.

096. Mokele-Mbembe

It is believed that the dinosaurs went extinct 66 million years ago. But could some of them have survived in the jungles of Africa?

The legend of Mokele-Mbembe comes from the folklore of the indigenous peoples of Central Africa, in particular the Baka and Bantu tribes. The creature is said to be a large, long-necked reptile with a body like that of an elephant, which is quite similar to certain species of dinosaur. Mokele-Mbembe is believed to live in remote areas that outsiders cannot easily enter, such as the dense jungles and swamps of the Congo Basin.

Since the early 20th century, many expeditions have gone into the Congo Basin in search of Mokele-Mbembe, drawn by reports of sightings and encounters with the elusive creature. While some of these expeditions have come up with tantalizing clues, like signs in the brush of a large creature passing by and even possible footprints, definitive proof of the creature itself remains to be found.

Mokele-Mbembe holds a unique place in the field of cryptozoology (the study of hidden or undiscovered animals). While skeptics have dismissed the legend as just that—a legend—or people mistaking known species like elephants for the mythical beast, those who believe that Mokele-Mbembe is real argue that the creature might be part of a group of dinosaurs that somehow survived extinction. Perhaps they even evolved from these ancient beasts to adapt to life in the heart of the Congo Basin.

The legend of Mokele-Mbembe has deep cultural significance for the tribes of Central Africa, who see the creature as a sacred guardian of the natural world. Stories of Mokele-Mbembe have been passed down through generations, mostly in the form of cautionary tales about why it is important to respect and preserve the wilderness and those who live within it.

Although they have not succeeded so far, adventurers continue to search the Congo Basin for concrete evidence of the creature, fueled by a fascination with dinosaurs and unknown creatures. Is Mokele-Mbembe a relic from the age of the dinosaurs, or just a figment of imagination? Either way, it is a source of curiosity and wonder for cryptozoologists around the world.

097. The Taos Hum

Since the early 1990s, residents of Taos, New Mexico, have reported hearing a mysterious, low-pitched sound known as the Taos Hum. Described as a faint, persistent buzz, the noise has also been compared to the sound of a distant diesel engine idling, or a low-frequency tremor in the ground. In the years since, the same kind of hum has been heard in cities around the world, from the Windsor Hum in Ontario, Canada to the Auckland Hum in Auckland, New Zealand.

The Taos Hum has been heard by as many as 2% of the population in Taos, with middle-aged people being more likely to hear it than others. People have found they could move away from the hum and hear it become fainter, and its range is estimated to be around 30 miles. Although this suggests that the hum has a source, it has yet to be found.

There is, of course, some skepticism as to whether the Taos Hum is an actual sound, but many theories have been suggested to explain it. Some propose that it may be caused by seismic activity somewhere underground, or the movement of groundwater. Others think the hum may be a side effect of industrial plants in the area. Some even propose that it's an effect of hearing conditions like tinnitus, or that it is purely psychological.

After decades of investigation, the true cause of the Taos Hum remains a mystery. All efforts to pinpoint the source of the noise have failed so far. For those affected by the Taos Hum, the constant noise has caused frustration, anxiety, and even some medical issues like headaches and insomnia. The distressing effects of the hum have led to calls for more research into locating its origins, in order to find a way to reduce the discomfort it causes.

098. The Giant Snake of the Congo

During a 1980 interview with the British TV Show *Mysterious World*, a Belgian Air Force Colonel named Remy Van Lierde made one of the more extraordinary claims in the history of cryptozoology. He claimed that in 1959, while flying over the Katanga Province in Congo by helicopter, he saw a greenish-brown snake that was nearly 50 feet long!

Van Lierde said that he dipped the helicopter lower to investigate the beast, at which point it raised its neck about 10 feet high to size up the helicopter as prey. It had a head like that of a very large horse, with a triangular jaw. Van Lierde then pulled the helicopter away for fear of his safety, but not before his companion in the helicopter managed to capture a photograph of the creature.

Other than Van Lierde's account, however, there is little evidence that such a massive snake exists in the Congo Basin. Even the photograph that was obtained by Van Lierde is grainy and in black-and-white, so was not adequate proof for investigators and adventurers. Later expeditions in search of the giant snake have not revealed any further evidence, and whether it really exists is a question yet to be answered.

Skeptics have dismissed the claims by Van Lierde as a hoax, or possibly a misrepresentation of some other creature. Scientists have suggested that the snake he saw might have been the African Rock Python, the largest species of snake known to live in the region. However, the African Rock Python has been recorded at 20 feet long at most—well below the length of the 50-foot beast that Van Lierde claimed to have seen.

Although there is a lack of proof that it exists, the giant snake of the Congo has captured the imagination of adventurers and cryptozoologists since Van Lierde spoke of his encounter. As more expeditions plumb the depths of the Congo Basin in search of its many secrets, perhaps the truth of the 50-foot serpent will be revealed someday!

099. The Phantom Island of Bermeja

The island of Bermeja was first discovered in the early 16th century by Spanish explorers, who then charted it on maps of the Gulf of Mexico. A rocky outcrop with a distinct red color (the word *bermeja* is Spanish for "reddish"), Bermeja was said to lie approximately 80 miles northwest of the Yucatán Peninsula, and was used as a landmark for sailors to navigate the region.

It was a prominent place on maps of the Caribbean for centuries after, but Bermeja became a source of great confusion in the 20th century, when several trips to the area found that the island had vanished! Even bigger and more thorough expeditions conducted by Mexican and American naval authorities have failed to find any trace of Bermeja since.

What could have happened to the island? The disappearance of Bermeja has given rise to many conspiracy theories, with some even suggesting that it was deliberately removed from maps by government agencies like the CIA or large corporations, for political or economic reasons. These ideas have led to rumors of secret military operations, drilling for oil, or other cover-ups that have only added to the intrigue of Bermeja's fate.

Geological surveys and satellite imagery of the Gulf of Mexico have given some clues about the possible fate of Bermeja, though. Some researchers think that the island may have been eroded over time, eventually sinking beneath the waves and down to the depths of the ocean. Another possibility is that it was shifted by plate tectonics.

Without any physical evidence to explain where Bermeja is now, the mystery of the vanishing island continues to intrigue researchers around the world. Whether it was brought down by natural forces, a victim of human intervention, or simply a map-making error that was somehow never fixed, the truth behind Bermeja's disappearance has yet to be discovered.

100. Remote Viewing

Remote viewing is the ability to see or get information about a distant, obscured target using extra-sensory perception (ESP) or "psychic" abilities. Simply put, it means viewing a target from a remote distance, which explains the name. Those who believe in remote viewing claim that it allows people to access information beyond the limits of their five senses by tapping into a kind of universal consciousness, or "field" of this information.

The practice of remote viewing has ancient roots, often showing up in occult or spiritual practices found in cultures around the world. However, it gained renewed interest in the 20th century with the new field of parapsychology (the study of paranormal events, particularly those involving the mind) and the study of psychic phenomena by researcher Joseph Banks Rhine.

Remote viewing got a second boost in popularity during the Cold War era, when it was reportedly used by intelligence agencies like the CIA and KGB for many of their operations. Project Stargate, a classified program run by the US government from the 1970s to the 1990s, was reported to have trained military personnel to use remote viewing to gather intelligence on targets of interest. One of the project's rare successes was the psychic finding of a Soviet spy plane that was lost in 1976. The project even studied famous magician and apparent psychic Uri Geller for a time!

Despite the overall failure of programs like Project Stargate, remote viewing has still been the subject of extensive research, even though the results from the experiments are considered by most of the scientific community to have little value.

The mystery of remote viewing raises some deep questions about how our consciousness can interact with the physical world. While new theories have suggested that remote viewing may involve some newer scientific discoveries, such as quantum effects, the truth behind psychic abilities like remote viewing is still unknown.

101. The Loch-Ness Monster

Some call it a survivor from the age of the dinosaurs, others say it is an overly famous floating log. Who or what is Nessie?

From as early as the 6th century CE, there have been tales in Scottish folklore of a mysterious aquatic creature lurking in the depths of the Loch Ness lake in the Scottish Highlands. Described as a large, long-necked creature with humps protruding from the water, the Loch Ness Monster (affectionately called "Nessie" by the Scottish) has captured the imagination of the public for generations, with many believing it could be a descendant of ancient sea serpents or some other mythical creature.

Loch Ness Monster sightings began in 1933, when a sudden series of encounters with Nessie were reported by various people. The most famous of these sightings was by George Spicer and his wife, who saw the creature casually cross the road in front of their car! This sparked widespread interest in the creature, and since then, hundreds of eyewitness accounts, photographs, and even videos appearing to show the elusive monster have fueled worldwide speculation about its existence.

In spite of all of the above, though, concrete evidence that the Loch Ness Monster exists has yet to be found. Several scientific investigations have been conducted with sonar scans, underwater cameras, and DNA sampling of the waters of Loch Ness, but all have failed to conclusively prove that a large unknown creature lives under the surface of the loch.

Researchers and skeptics have come up with various explanations for Loch Ness Monster sightings. Some think that the witnesses might have actually seen a seal or a floating log and believed it to be Nessie after hearing about the legend. Others suggest that many of the sightings are hoaxes for the purpose of fame or money.

Those who believe that the Loch Ness Monster exists think that Nessie may be related to prehistoric marine reptiles, such as plesiosaurs (which were also large and long-necked), that somehow survived the extinction that killed the dinosaurs 66 million years ago.

Whether a real creature lurking in the depths of Loch Ness or a figment of the collective imagination of those in the vicinity, the Loch Ness Monster has become a cultural icon, inspiring countless books, movies, documentaries, and tourist attractions dedicated to the elusive creature. The annual Loch Ness Monster Day, celebrated on April 21st, the day the most famous photo of Nessie was published in *The Daily Mail*, draws visitors from around the world to the shores of Loch Ness to commemorate Nessie's legacy and keep the legend alive. One day, maybe some of these devotees will even catch a glimpse of the star cryptid itself!

CONCLUSION

We have now delved deep into history to learn about its unsolved mysteries and have found ancient riddles whose answers are likely lost to time, along with monuments whose construction is incredible even by modern standards. From the Pyramids of Giza to the Nazca Lines, much of the past continues to elude our understanding.

As we moved through the centuries, we learned of mystifying figures like Jack the Ripper and The Man in the Iron Mask, as well as curious events like the Miracle of the Sun and the Dancing Plague. Even in the last century, with better technology and a wider grasp of how our world works, cryptic figures like the Zodiac Killer and vanishing acts like that of DB Cooper still manage to leave their mark on our collective imagination. And it's clear that science has innumerable mysteries left to solve, from the real nature of Dark Matter to the origins of the Moon and beyond.

For all that we still don't fully understand, one thing is clear: human curiosity is limitless. It is our desire to know more, to understand the way things work, and to solve the most enigmatic mysteries, that pushes us forward as a society.

When it comes to mysteries, finding answers often means exploring places that may be unfamiliar and unknown, like the depths of the Amazon or the vastness of the Sahara, or even new states of mind. It is in these unknown places that we have our best chance to find the answers we seek, whether it is the truth behind extraterrestrial life or the secrets of ancient civilizations.

So as you close the pages of this humble little trivia book, try to stay curious and open-minded, and don't be put off by the unknown as you embark on your own adventures to find answers. The mysteries we've talked about here are unsolved, but there have been countless others that have been figured out, some even in just the last few years. The world has many more secrets to be uncovered by the brightest minds of the future, so you might even be one of those solving the next great mystery!

Remember, each time a mystery is solved, we learn more about life and its meaning, and humanity is encouraged to maintain a sense of wonder and continue its search for answers to all that is yet unknown.

A SHORT MESSAGE FROM THE AUTHOR

Hey, are you enjoying the book? I'd love to hear your thoughts!

Many readers do not know how hard reviews are to come by, and how much they help an author.

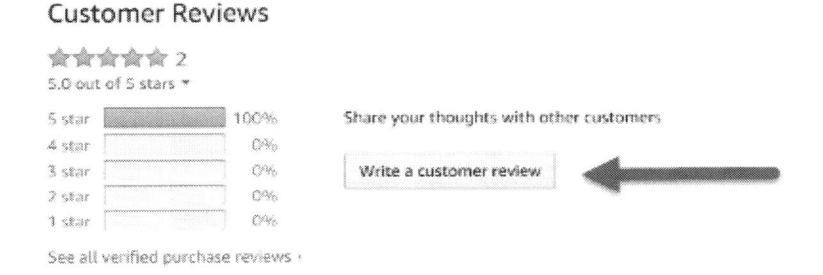

I would be incredibly grateful if you could take just 60 seconds to write a brief review on Amazon, even if it's just a few sentences!

Thank you for taking the time to share your thoughts!

Your review will genuinely make a difference for me and help gain exposure for my work.

Thank you

REFERENCES

ABC/Wires. (2016, April 15). *Malaysia Airlines MH370: One year on, still no trace of plane that disappeared with 239 people onboard | Australia Plus.* Web.archive.org. https://web.archive.org/web/20160415142156/http://australiaplus.com/international/2015-03-08/malaysia-airlines-mh370-one-year-on-still-no-trace-of-plane-that-disappeared-with-239-people-onboard/1422759

Arun, K., Gudennavar, S. B., & Sivaram, C. (2017). Dark matter, dark energy, and alternate models: A review. *Advances in Space Research*, *60*(1), 166–186. https://doi.org/10.1016/j.asr.2017.03.043

Aschwanden, M. (2006). Coronal Heating. *Springer EBooks*, 355–406. https://doi.org/10.1007/3-540-30766-4_9

Aveni, A. F. (1990). *The Lines of Nazca.* American Philosophical Society Press.

Barker, R. (1988). *Great Mysteries of the Air.* Javelin.

BBC NEWS | Science/Nature | Riddle of "Baghdad's batteries." (2009). Bbc.co.uk. http://news.bbc.co.uk/2/hi/science/nature/2804257.stm

Begg, P. (2013). *Jack the Ripper: The Definitive History.* Taylor and Francis.

Begg, P. (2014). *Mary Celeste.* Routledge.

Bennett, J. S. (2012). *When the Sun Danced: Myth, Miracles, and Modernity in Early Twentieth-Century Portugal.* University Of Virginia Press.

Blanke, O., Landis, T., Spinelli, L., & Seeck, M. (2004). Out-of-body experience and autoscopy of neurological origin. *Brain: A Journal of Neurology, 127*(Pt 2), 243–258. https://doi.org/10.1093/brain/awh040

Boerner, H., & Williams, E. R. (2019). *Ball lightning : a popular guide to a longstanding mystery in atmospheric electricity.* Springer Nature Switzerland AG.

Bowen, C. (1967). The Mystery of the Morro do Vintem. *Flying Saucer Review, 13*(2), 11.

Brannen, P. (2017). *The Ends of the World: volcanic apocalypses, lethal oceans, and our quest to understand Earth's past mass extinctions.* Ecco, An Imprint Of Harpercollins Publishers.

Brooks, M. (2005, March 16). *13 things that do not make sense.* New Scientist. https://www.newscientist.com/article/mg18524911-600-13-things-that-do-not-make-sense/

Bugliosi, V. (2007). *Reclaiming History : the assassination of President John F. Kennedy.* Norton.

Campbell, J. (1990). *Transformations of Myth Through Time.* Harper Perennial.

Chandler, N. (2019, December 30). *What's Really Going on at the "Dog Suicide Bridge"?* HowStuffWorks. https://science.howstuffworks.com/science-vs-myth/unexplained-phenomena/dog-suicide-bridge.htm

Clay, R., & Dawson, B. (1998). *Cosmic Bullets.* Addison-Wesley Longman.

Clayton, P. A., & Price, M. (2015). *The seven wonders of the ancient world.* Routledge.

Curry, A. (2021, August 17). *An immense mystery older than Stonehenge*. Www.bbc.com. https://www.bbc.com/travel/article/20210815-an-immense-mystery-older-than-stonehenge

Diehl, R. A. (2006). *The Olmecs: America's first civilization*. Thames & Hudson.

Dove, P. (2020). *The Disappearance of Jimmy Hoffa*. Manor Books, New York.

Duffy, E. (2017, April 20). *Secret Knowledge—or a Hoax?* The New York Review of Books. https://www.nybooks.com/articles/2017/04/20/voynich-manuscript-secret-knowledge-or-hoax/

Elborough, T. (2019). *Atlas of Vanishing Places*. White Lion Publishing.

Fanthorpe, L., & Fanthorpe, P. (1997). *The World's Greatest Unsolved Mysteries*. Dundurn.

Fears, J. R. (1978). *Atlantis, fact or fiction?* Bloomington: Indiana University Press.

Flaherty, T. H. (1992). *Unsolved crimes*. Time-Life Books.

Forgan, D. (2019). *Solving Fermi's Paradox*. Cambridge University Press.

Foster, C. (2007). *Tracking the Ark of the Covenant*. Monarch.

Fox, D. (2016). What sparked the Cambrian explosion? *Nature, 530*(7590), 268–270. https://doi.org/10.1038/530268a

Freed, L., & Fetzer, R. (2021, August 25). *Has the anonymous author of the infamous Circleville letters been unmasked?*

Www.cbsnews.com. https://www.cbsnews.com/news/circleville-letters-author-unmask/

Freeth, T. (2009). Decoding an Ancient Computer. *Scientific American, 301*(6), 76–83. https://doi.org/10.1038/scientificamerican1209-76

Furneaux, R., & Dauger, E. (1954). *The Man Behind the Mask.* London: Cassell.

Gibson, J. W. (2010). *Judge Crater, the Missingest Person.* Dog Ear Publishing.

Gordon, H. (1988). *Extrasensory Deception.* MacMillan of Canada.

Gould, R. T. (1976). *The Loch Ness monster and others.* Citadel Press.

Gray, G. (2012). *Skyjack: The Hunt for D.B. Cooper.* Broadway Paperbacks.

Gray, R. H. (2012). *The Elusive Wow: Searching for Extraterrestrial Intelligence.* Palmer Square Press.

Griaule, M., & Dieterlen, G. (1986). *The Pale Fox.* Continuum Foundation.

Gunn, Dr. A. (2023, June 17). *A mysterious force keeps destroying the Universe's lithium. And scientists don't know why.* Www.sciencefocus.com. https://www.sciencefocus.com/science/lithium-shortage-universe

Haag, M. (2013). *The Tragedy of the Templars.* Harper Collins.

Hale, T. (2023, May 30). *Legend Of Congo's 15-Meter Snake Is Cryptozoology's Most Ludicrous Tale.* IFLScience.

https://www.iflscience.com/legend-of-congos-15-meter-snake-is-cryptozoologys-most-ludicrous-tale-69165

Harris, J. (2023). *Without Trace: the Last Voyages of Eight Ships*. Canelo.

Haughton, B. (n.d.). *Omm Sety - Priestess of Ancient Egypt by Brian Haughton*. Http://Brian-Haughton.com/. Retrieved April 9, 2024, from http://brian-haughton.com/ancient-mysteries-articles/omm-sety-priestess-of-ancient-egypt/

Hillpot, J. (2023, February 14). *The Booby Traps of Qin Shi Huang's Tomb: Fact, Fiction or Something Even Better?* Discover Magazine. https://www.discovermagazine.com/the-sciences/the-booby-traps-of-qin-shi-huangs-tomb-fact-fiction-or-something-even-better

Katz, H. (2010). *Cold Cases*. Bloomsbury Publishing USA.

Khatri, V. (2012). *World Famous Treasures Lost and Found*. Pustak Mahal.

Kingston, J. (2023, November 15). *In 1957, Jacqueline & Joanna were killed in a car accident. The next year they were "reincarnated"*. Mamamia. https://www.mamamia.com.au/pollock-twins/

Kober, A. E. (1948). The Minoan Scripts: Fact and Theory. *American Journal of Archaeology, 52*(1), 82–103. https://doi.org/10.2307/500554

Kurkjian, S. (2015). *Master Thieves*. PublicAffairs.

Lawler, A. (2019). *SECRET TOKEN : Obsession, deceit, and the search for the Lost Colony of Roanoke*. New York: Doubleday.

Lämmerzahl, C., Dittus, H., & Preuss, O. (2006). Is the physics within the Solar system really understood? *ArXiv (Cornell University)*. https://doi.org/10.48550/arxiv.gr-qc/0604052

Leventhall, H. G. (2004). Low frequency noise and annoyance. *Noise & Health*, *6*(23), 59–72.

Light, N. (2008, May 15). *Hidden Discourses of Race: Imagining Europeans in China*. Web.archive.org. https://web.archive.org/web/20080515210246/http://homepages.utoledo.edu/nlight/uyghhst.htm

Lorenzi, R. (2016, March 4). *The quest for Cambyses' lost army : Discovery News*. Web.archive.org. https://web.archive.org/web/20160304190029/http://news.discovery.com/history/ancient-egypt/the-quest-for-cambyses-lost-army.htm

Lotus, B. (2020, November 13). *Bigger Than Dinner Plates:* Creatures. https://medium.com/creatures/bigger-than-dinner-plates-e938e9157501

Lupin, G. (2023). *Medieval Devil's Bible Codex Gigas*. Independently Published.

Malone, C., & Bernard, N. S. (2002). *Stonehenge*. Oxford University Press.

Mariette, A. (1877). *The Monuments of Upper Egypt*. Mansfield & Dearborn.

Matthews, R. (2007). *Ancient Worlds*. Wayland Publishing.

Matton, G., & Jébrak, M. (2014). The "eye of Africa" (Richat dome, Mauritania): An isolated Cretaceous alkaline–hydrothermal complex. *Journal of African Earth Sciences*, *97*(97), 109–124. https://doi.org/10.1016/j.jafrearsci.2014.04.006

McCloskey, K. (2013). *Mountain of the Dead : the Dyatlov Pass Incident*. The History Press.

McClure, R., & Heffron, J. (2009). *Coral Castle*. Ternary Publishing LLC.

McIntosh, G. C. (2012). *Piri Reis Map of 1513*. University of Georgia Press.

Medievalists.net. (2023, April 23). *The Emerald Tablet and the Origins of Chemistry*. Medievalists.net. https://www.medievalists.net/2023/04/the-emerald-tablet-and-the-origins-of-chemistry/

Melia, F. (2003). *The Edge of Infinity: Supermassive Black Holes in the Universe*. Cambridge University Press.

Merwe, M. V. D. (2014, December 11). *The Elisa Lam mystery: Still no answers*. Daily Maverick. https://www.dailymaverick.co.za/article/2014-12-12-the-elisa-lam-mystery-still-no-answers/

Morris, T. (2010). *Roswell Connection*. Lulu.com.

Napier, J. R. (1974). *Bigfoot*. Newton Abbot: Readers Union.

Nast, C. (2005, September 12). *The Lost City of Z*. The New Yorker. https://www.newyorker.com/magazine/2005/09/19/the-lost-city-of-z

Nazaryan, A. (2017, February 2). *California's Lost Viking Treasure Ship*. Newsweek. https://www.newsweek.com/2017/02/10/lost-viking-treasure-ship-california-colorado-desert-547251.html

Nicastro, F., Krongold, Y., Mathur, S., & Elvis, M. (2017). A decade of warm hot intergalactic medium searches: Where do we stand and where do we go? *Astronomische Nachrichten, 338*(2-3), 281–286. https://doi.org/10.1002/asna.201713343

Nickell, J. (1992). *Ambrose Bierce is Missing and Other Historical Mysteries*. University Press of Kentucky.

Niu, C.-H. ., Aggarwal, K., Li, D., Zhang, X., Chatterjee, S., Tsai, C.-W. ., Yu, W., Law, C. J., Burke-Spolaor, S., Cordes, J. M., Zhang, Y.-K. ., Ocker, S. K., Yao, J.-M. ., Wan, P., Feng, Y., Niino, Y., Bochenek, C., Cruces, M., Connor, L., & Jiang, J.-A. . (2022). A repeating fast radio burst associated with a persistent radio source. *Nature, 606*(7916), 873–877. https://doi.org/10.1038/s41586-022-04755-5

Ouzts, C. (2022, July 11). *Georgia Guidestones*. New Georgia Encyclopedia. https://www.georgiaencyclopedia.org/articles/history-archaeology/georgia-guidestones/

Paine, L. (2015). *The sea and civilization : a maritime history of the world*. Vintage Books.

Pappas, S. (2017, September 21). *Plate Tectonics May Have Begun a Billion Years After Earth's Birth*. Livescience.com. https://www.livescience.com/60478-plate-tectonics-gets-new-age.html

Perkins, S. (2009). Story One: A century later, scientists still study Tunguska: Asteroid or comet blamed for Siberian blast of 1908. *Science News, 173*(19), 5–6. https://doi.org/10.1002/scin.2008.5591731904

PeruTravelTrends. (2013, April 29). *Visit Sacsayhuaman to ponder an awesome megalithic mystery*. Www.fertur-Travel.com. https://www.fertur-travel.com/blog/2013/visit-sacsayhuaman-to-ponder-an-awesome-megalithic-mystery/6544/

Picknett, L., & Prince, C. (2000). *Turin Shroud*. Harper-Collins.

Pinkney, J. (2003). *Great Australian Mysteries: Unsolved, Unexplained, Unknown*. The Five Mile Press Pty Ltd.

Powell, J. L. (2022). Peer review and the pillar of salt: a case study. *Research Ethics, 19*(1), 174701612211314. https://doi.org/10.1177/17470161221131491

Radford, B. (2013, August 14). *Mokele-Mbembe: The Search for a Living Dinosaur*. Livescience.com. https://www.livescience.com/38871-mokele-mbembe.html

Ramsay, R. H. (1972). *No Longer on the Map*. Viking Adult.

Rosen, D., & Caldwell, M. (2010). Asleep: the Forgotten Epidemic That Remains One of Medicine's Greatest Mysteries. *Journal of Clinical Sleep Medicine, 06*(03), 299–299. https://doi.org/10.5664/jcsm.27831

Shanks, H. (1999). *The mystery and meaning of the Dead Sea Scrolls*. Random House.

Shelley, P. B. (1826). *Miscellaneous and Posthumous Poems of Percy Bysshe Shelley*. London: W. Benbow.

Silver, K. (2019, October 26). *BBC - Earth - Where did the Moon come from?* Web.archive.org. https://web.archive.org/web/20191026002954/http://www.bbc.com/earth/story/20150617-where-did-the-moon-come-from

Simpson, J., & Roud, S. (2000). *A Dictionary of English Folklore*. Oxford University Press, USA.

Sims, L., Dodd, E., Jackson, I., Woodcock, J., & Chisholm, J. (2014). *A visitor's guide to ancient Egypt*. Usborne.

Stewart, G. B. (2009). *The Bermuda Triangle*. Capstone.

Straw, M. J. (2002). *Loretto: the sisters and their Santa Fe chapel*. Museum Of New Mexico Press.

Sullivan, R. (2018). *The Curse of Oak Island*. Atlantic Monthly Press.

The New York Times. (1994, August 20). Mystery Blobs Were Once Alive. *Observer-Reporter*.

Thornton, T. (2020). More on a Murder: The Deaths of the "Princes in the Tower", and Historiographical Implications for the Regimes of Henry VII and Henry VIII. *History, 106*(369), 4–25. https://doi.org/10.1111/1468-229x.13100

Ucko, P. J. (2005). *Theory in Archaeology*. Routledge.

Waller, J. (2009). *Dancing Plague : The Strange, True Story of an Extraordinary Illness*. Sourcebooks, Inc.

Waters, D. (2021, October 30). The Mystery of the "Mad Gasser of Mattoon" Who Terrorized an Illinois Town. *Washington Post*. https://www.washingtonpost.com/history/2021/10/30/mad-gasser-mattoon-illinois-mystery/

Weatherford, J. (2012). *Genghis Khan and the Making of the Modern World*. Three Rivers Press, Ulaanbaatar. (Original work published 2004)

Weinberg, S. (2011). *Dreams of a Final Theory*. Vintage.

Winstone, H. V. F. (2006). *Howard Carter and the discovery of the tomb of Tutankhamun*. Barzan Publishing.

Wolfgang, V. (1978). *The gold of El Dorado: The quest for the golden man*. Granada Pub.

Printed in Great Britain
by Amazon